BELIEF

BELIEF

✳

Joan Bakewell

EAST RENFREWSHIRE COUNCIL	
0527815	
Bertrams	17.07.05
202	£12.99

Duckworth Overlook

London • New York • Woodstock

First published in 2005 by
Duckworth Overlook

LONDON
90-93 Cowcross Street
London EC1M 6BF
inquiries@duckworth-publishers.co.uk
www.ducknet.co.uk

NEW YORK
The Overlook Press
141 Wooster Street
New York, NY 10012

WOODSTOCK
The Overlook Press
One Overlook Drive
Woodstock, NY 12498
www.overlookpress.com
[for individual orders and bulk sales in the United States,
please contact our Woodstock office]

By arrangement with the BBC

The BBC logo is a registered trade mark of the British
Broadcasting Corporation and is used under licence.

BBC logo © BBC 1996

A CIP catalogue record for this book is available
from the British Library

ISBN 0 7156 3378 3 (UK)
ISBN 1-58567-697-7 (US)

Typeset by Ray Davies
Printed in Great Britain by
CPD, Wales

Contents

Introduction   7

Acknowledgements   11

1. Antony Gormley: '… a parallel universe'   13

2. James Lovelock: 'The odds are quite high that
    we'll revert back to being tribal carnivores'   24

3. Terry Eagleton: 'A synthesis of Christianity and
    Marxism makes a lot of intellectual sense'   38

4. Karen Armstrong: 'Follow the Bliss'   51

5. Anish Kapoor: 'I feel very passionately that I do
    not have anything to say…'   63

6. Rowan Williams: '… the pebble dropped into
    the pool'   72

7. Paul Davies: '… the universe is about something
    … it is not just arbitrary and absurd.'   84

8. Father Timothy Radcliffe: '… the pilgrimage
    to truth'   96

9. David Puttnam: 'Film allows you insights into
    your own ethical being'   107

10. James Macmillan: 'Inspiration has a divine
    dimension'   119

11. Amy Tan: 'A spiritual meditation'   130

12. Robert Winston: 'Playing God … the highest thing
    we can do'   142

13. Ziauddin Sardar: 'The beginning of knowledge'   155

14. Philip Pullman: 'Moral codes are a very interesting
    example of how religions get things wrong'   169

15. Minette Walters: 'More comfortable to be an
    atheist'   183

16. John Tavener: 'Primordial depth'   195

17. Richard Dawkins: 'In a sense humans have
    emancipated themselves from natural selection.'   206

18. Andrew Motion: 'The value of the numinous'   220

19. Jeanette Winterson: 'I am not a Christian, but I am
    one of the faithful'   228

20. John O'Donohue: 'Landscape is the first scripture'   240

�֎

JOAN BAKEWELL

Introduction

✻

In the summer of 2001 I found myself in discussion about the role and scope of the BBC's Religious Department. I had been contributing to its programmes over some 30 years. Throughout that time I had seen its attitudes to faith and belief change, just as those of the country at large had done. Back in the beginning in 1928, under the unflinching leadership of Lord Reith, the BBC had no doubt about the central role of Christianity within its remit. Documents from that time speak of the BBC's 'doing its best to prevent any decay of Christianity in a nominally Christian country', and 'giving new life and meaning to the traditionally Christian character of the British people'. In the post-war years, any sliver of doubt was quickly crushed by a strengthening of resolve: in 1948 the then Director General, William Haley, declared 'some people may ask whether British Broadcasting is neutral where Christian values are concerned. Of course it is not. ...We are citizens of a Christian country and the BBC – an institution set up by the state – bases its policy upon a positive attitude towards Christian values.'

By the 1960s when I made my first programmes, the BBC had largely passed into the hands of a generation of secular arts graduates, but the Religious Department was still fulfilling its primarily Christian role. Its head had always, with one exception, been an ordained cleric of the Church of England and that was to remain the case until 2000. It was not until 2001 that the first television professional was appointed to the job. In 2000 the Department had been renamed the Department of Religion and Ethics. Thus has one of the long-standing core functions of British broadcasting gradually evolved into something more appropriate for these times.

By the 1990s, BBC Religion, increasingly concerned about its obligations to the beliefs of ethnic minority communities, had conducted an enquiry into what people say they believe. It findings were strangely disquieting. The saddest outcome of the survey was the conclusion that a majority of the population are people of 'vague faith'. This concept – vague faith – suggests those who when asked whether they believe in God or not, answer in essentially unsophisticated terms – 'Well, yes, I feel there has to be something, doesn't there.' 'I suppose something must have started it all, so, yes, I suppose I do.' These were not the conclusions of a people who had spent a great deal of time in rigorous appraisal of their beliefs. This was not a nation in the grip of religious profundities. Into this evolving scheme of things, I threw my few pence of comment. I wanted to push an idea for an entirely individual concept of faith, and to hear its many voices. The *Belief* series was born. Since 2001 I have conducted some 47 conversations, of which 20 are presented here.

During that time, there has been accelerating change in the world. Religion has swept back onto both the domestic and the international agenda. Christianity in Britain has been gripped by continuing convulsions. The Catholic hierarchy has suffered a grievous loss of respect and trust following its paedophile scandals; the Church of England remains embattled over the issues of women in the priesthood and the homosexual clergy. At the same time the evangelical wing of the Christian faith is enjoying a rapid and passionate expansion. The Alpha Course – a proselytising crusade aimed at the affluent middle classes – and the black-majority Gospel and Charismatic churches, have boosted their numbers and injected a new enthusiasm into Christian worship. An evangelical President of the United States has entered his second term of office with religious observance firmly entrenched in White House procedures, and with a cabinet of fellow Christians who thread their pronouncements of international policy with an Old Testament vocabulary of good and evil, and unhappy references to crusades and a clash of civilisations.

In parallel the rise of fundamentalism throughout the world is now driving the international agenda. An increasing number of Muslim countries have made shariah law the legal framework of the state. Political loyalties are increasingly tied to the profession of religious credos; minority faiths come under attack simply for being different. Asians in Britain ask to be identified as Hindu or Muslim or Sikh. Suddenly what you believe has become part of your public identity. Religious allegiances are becoming dangerously allied with a tendency towards tribalism.

At such a time it is good to listen to the thoughtful and considered beliefs of individuals of intelligence and reputation. Beliefs are not simply the codes and credos of religions and sects. Indeed it is clearly the case that individuals – even those espousing the orthodoxy of an established faith – bring to its tenets their personality and intelligence which renders their personal belief unique. It is impossible to police the human conscience. So even among a number of people professing the same religion, their actual beliefs will be born of their individual lives and circumstance. So it is within these pages. Here are people chosen simply for themselves, not as representative of faiths or to demonstrate any clash of ideologies. And, regardless of changing world events, their beliefs remain strong as the basis for judgement and action.

People can believe in many things; in horoscopes, in crystals, in ley lines, scientology, spiritualism, witchcraft, the transmigration of souls, or indeed any of the 12 or so strongly-established and widely-observed world religions. Or they can have beliefs shaped by a more rational and scientific outlook; a belief in the values of this life: justice, humanity, beauty, art. It is rare to find anyone who sets aside the question, saying they have no beliefs at all. And in large part, until recently, it was widely felt that people were free to choose and follow their own beliefs.

What emerges is more complicated that that. Children are born into already well-established and shared belief systems. Their first experience of trust and love comes with the ideas of parents whom they have neither reason nor capacity to doubt. So our first beliefs are implicit in our background. Beyond the home, they will be reinforced by the community of belief in which they are grounded. Thus early and thoroughly do we grow unwittingly absorbing attitudes, ethics, stories and beliefs. In his *On Liberty*, John Stuart Mill wrote: 'He who does anything because it is the custom, makes no choice.' It is only as our interaction with the world grows and develops that we come to exercise our freedom to explore and develop new ideas. The stories within these pages demonstrate just such choices being made. Each individual journey is unique and fascinating. What they say can challenge our own beliefs, perhaps grown routine with habit. Here are new insights into the many and diverse beliefs individuals have about the world.

Acknowledgements

❖

This book owes its existence to the BBC Radio 3 programme, *Belief*, an on-going series in which I interview people of diverse views and reflective temperament about what they believe about the world and things beyond. I could not do this without the commitment of Radio 3 itself, and the BBC's Department of Religion and Ethics. Most particularly I owe a debt of gratitude to my producers of the programmes: Anna Cox, Tim Pemberton, Janet MacClarty, Rosie Dawson, Karen Maurice, Norman Winter, who also gave valuable assistance with their publication.

❖

1

ANTONY GORMLEY

'… a parallel universe'

Antony Gormley is one of Britain's foremost sculptors. After Cambridge, he studied at London's Central School of Art, Goldsmith's College, and The Slade School of Art. Throughout his career he has used moulds of his own body as an archetype, the starting-point for his continuing exploration of the relationship of the human and its context. His most famous works include the Angel of the North *which towers 20 metres high beside the motorway approach to Tyneside,* Field, *made up of some 40,000 small terracotta figures, and* Quantum Cloud, *created to stand beside the Thames at the Millennium Dome. He has made large-scale installations for Cuxhaven in Germany and the Royal Academy in London. He won the Turner Prize in 1994 and the South Bank Prize in 1999.*

I was brought up a Catholic in which everything either had an answer or was a mystery for which we should not seek to have a definite answer in this life. I've tried not to have belief. I've tried to make things that deal with my uncertainties, but also with my faith. I think faith is rather different from belief. Belief is a lack of knowledge, but faith is something that we can posit within human life and human consciousness as an evolving process. And I think that's where art and sculpture come. Art can provide objects of which their principal value is that they are instruments through which we can know our-selves better.

You are the youngest of seven siblings: what was that like as a child?

Our family was run a bit like an organisation, and I think religion was part of the rules. Being the youngest is quite a problem. From the older children's point of view you're horri-bly spoilt and indulged in ways that they weren't. From your point of view, everything has already been said, everything has already been done and there is very little to add. I can just remember very early on feeling that I had to make my own place, I had to find an alternative space where I could grow.

And the Catholic teaching offered very clear Catholic rules?

Yes. 'Why are you born?' ' I was born to serve God, to love him and ...', whatever it is. And I think that was in some sense almost interchangeable with the kind of family system. We had prayers at night and sometimes in the morning, and then, going to school, there was more of the same. And I look on it now as in a way a form of abuse. I know that sounds a little heavy, but there was a sense in which this was indoctrination, done in the name of love, but in fact was a form of emotional blackmail in which all of those things that I think human nature is very susceptible to – guilt and anxiety – were in some way used as forms of manipulation.

Did you feel very guilty yourself?

I think I was very profoundly affected by that religious environment. I attempted to have a very strong relationship with the Virgin Mary for instance, which I think is a common escape route from a more male and disciplining father God figure.

Did you talk to her?

Yes, I must have spent long hours on my knees in front of a plaster Virgin. I can hardly look at those images now without feeling a certain kind of sickness in the stomach. But there were a lot of moments of deep disappointment in the evolution of my relationship with Christianity, and I think the first was 'first communion'.

What happened?

There's something very moving I always think about look-ing at people's faces when they return from the altar, when they've taken the Holy Eucharist and there is some extraordi-nary transformation taking place and you seek signs of that in the transfiguration of their faces. I believed I could see that. And then it didn't happen for me and suddenly there was this extraordinary rite of passage, this moment of taking the host and going back to my pew and closing my eyes and there being just darkness and a sense that, oh goodness, actually nothing is going to happen.

Christianity also offers a code for living which, if you follow it and observe it, is enormously supportive. Did you accept that code and find it nourishing?

Basic Christian morality – 'love thy neighbour as thyself' – is absolutely a fundamental rule of Christian and all society. It's what helps life become liveable, and hopefully more than liveable, because it encourages empathy. But the fundamental image of Christianity I have problems with because it is to do with the denial of the body. I think that the crucifixion in some sense is also an expression of the fear of the body, in general as a sexual object. I suspect that's where I begin to part company with Christianity.

You went to Ampleforth, a leading Catholic public school.

While I was there I was a full participant. I regularly took the sacraments and I regularly went to confession, and I had a wonderful time at Ampleforth. I found that that was the first step of my liberation really from the rigours of home life. But I left the Church the minute I left Ampleforth.

And it was there that you began to really explore art and your love of art.

We did at least two periods of two-hour-long drawing sessions per week for the whole time that I was there. I won the school art prize a couple of times, and I painted a lot of pictures, some of which were bought by the school. So, immense support and immense encouragement at a very early age, which was very important. Art was always for me this zone where possibility was rife, where anything could happen. I would dash up there during the first break, start something off on a big piece of hardboard, throw lots of colours and maybe some earth together and swill it all about with some oil and then rush up before lunch to see what was going on in this chaotic canvas and then at the next possible opportunity go up there again. And it's still like that for me. I think that the zone of possibility that art offers is like a parallel universe.

When you gave up Catholicism did you find it a void? Did you feel emptied out?

No, I felt liberated. It was a wonderful time, so I'm afraid that Catholicism went with a lot of other things.

And what came in its place?

A very robust engagement with ideas about expanding your mind in all ways. I was interested in alternative religions,

I took my fair share of drugs, I did a bit of acting. And I began to travel. It was in the first long vacation at Cambridge that I went to India for the first time.

So you were a bit of a hippy?
   I was and still am. I am a hippy I think at heart.

Tell me what influence India had?
   I think that the real engagement happened after I left. When I arrived back in India at the beginning of 1972, I met S. N. Goenka who taught Vipasasana meditation and I think the minute that I started this form of very simple Buddhist meditation I made a connection with an experience that I'd had as a child. As a child in the 1950s I had to have my rest after lunch. I remember, when my eyes were closed, feeling this unbelievably claustrophobic space behind the eyes which would be almost suffocating, a matchbox-shaped darkness that was never big enough, and dwelling in that space. And slowly but surely that small claustrophobic matchbox darkness opening up and opening up until it was as big as deep space in which I was floating, and it went from liberation through to fear and then back into a kind of freeform floating. And I re-linked with that space in a deep way for the first time again through meditation in India and I think that is still the space that I am interested in. That's where all of these things that we used to call the soul, what we might now call imagination, dwell, and out of which everything comes in terms of consciousness.

I'm interested that you took instruction to access this depth of insight; a new set of rules perhaps or a technique.
   A very, very simple technique, a way of being still, a way of sitting and a way of leaving the distractions behind. In some

senses the twin powers of desire and aversion disappear along with the ego. When you sit still and watch what is actually happening, you realise that everything is in flux, that we are just a bundle of energy and that actually where we begin and end is not a very defined thing. It's a process. And it is possible to expand consciousness itself.

So you practice meditation every day …

Well it's become synonymous with the work. I use my body as the material out of which the work comes, and the process of being moulded is itself, I believe, a profoundly meditative experience where you have to be there completely. You have to be at one with your body, as the plaster is placed around you. And as the plaster heats up in the chemical reaction, as it is hardening, so you yourself can relax because this act of will is translated into this exoskeleton and its form then becomes the condition of your existence. It's a very extraordinary process and in a way it has become my meditation.

How long does it take?

An hour, an hour and a half.

Do you ever feel trapped? Have you ever been trapped?

It's happened once or twice. It happened early on when my wife had to go and answer the front door or the telephone or something. I was just standing there and this little bit of plaster just happened to fall in front of my breathing hole. I was going 'phhh, phhh' … to blow this thing away, to get it out, but I couldn't move because I was entirely encased. It kept sort of falling back and 'ugh' and I couldn't breathe, and that was panic. I almost blacked out. Vicken reappeared after about 10 minutes, but by that time I was fairly alarmed.

Your exposition of consciousness and where it ends, seems to be at odds with the figures you produce which are very clearly there, and not there. They are hard, rigid outlines of your body in different positions, sitting, standing, but also up in the ceiling or out at sea. Angel of the North *couldn't be more absolute in its presence. There is nothing confusing about the edges of the* Angel of the North. *Do you find that hard to reconcile?*

That's a very important question. As far as I am concerned, the works are not representations. They are testaments or witnesses to an existence. They are indexical evidence of where one particular body once was and by implication anybody could be. I am hoping that people will relate to them, because they're not representations, by asking much more fundamental questions, like 'what the hell is this thing?' 'What's it doing here?' 'how does it work?' and in some senses those questions then get returned by the mute objects and they have to reflexively ask themselves 'what am I doing here?' 'how do I work?' Empathy is one of the ways I think that you can relate to these works, even the *Angel*. The sense of their being an object isolated in space that might have less to do with art and more to do with life is part of how they work. That's why I've been very interested in using the beach, or a hilltop or places that are not confined by architecture. Because I think then the relationship between this human sign and everything that it is not, is much more manifest. And in a sense then the question of 'who it is' is much more open. It can be an image that anyone can inhabit.

You entered into a political minefield with a sculpture you did in 1987 called Derry Walls *which involved figures facing both ways, a comment on a very obvious rift in the community. Were you surprised at the effect it had?*

The sculpture for *Derry Walls* is a very specific work. It's two body cases that are crucified to each other, taking the central image of Christianity, the arms are stuck out at the side, the eyes are open, so that you can look through one set of eyes and out of the other at these two views, inside and outside the walls. The idea was to make a benign object that stated both the history and the present divided nature of this community, but to do it in such way where this central image of Christianity was reconfigured. The very fact that the work was attacked by both communities meant that it was doing its job. I saw it as a poultice. Here was this benign object that called to itself thoughts and feelings that might otherwise be expressed violently against other human beings. That's certainly what happened. In a sense it still remains for me one of my most beloved public works, because it's testing where art belongs, who it's for, what it can do. It's very unusual to see art on the front line of the human conflict like that.

You use the word 'poultice', and elsewhere you've said that you see art as a catalyst for healing. Is your art healing you? Is your art therapy?

Absolutely. I think that the basic 'doctor-heal-thyself' is absolutely to be applied to art. I think if art is not in some senses an instrument for its maker, how can it be an instrument for the rest of us. I'm absolutely certain that I couldn't live without it. It's the balancing mechanism in my life. I offer it to the rest of the world for whatever it's worth, and its only way of having worth is as a space. Even the most solid of my works, the three-quarter-of-a-tonne body forms; I think of them as a space, even if it is a materialised space. And I offer that as a space of possibility to the world. They are so very different from statues. They don't represent a particular person in the way that a statue does, and they don't represent a particular ideology or history, or narrative. They are about possibility and about potential.

Field is a very famous but very different kind of work because it is made up of some thousands of small figures, presumably designed by you but made by many people. I wonder if you see art as having a civic and moral role in society and community?

No, I think it's tribal basically. Art is one of the principal ways in which a community discovers itself and this is something that we've lost. *Field* takes a lot of making, and, the making is half of the work. It's very important it's a collective activity. It's very important that the form of each of those pieces is absolutely unique and comes not through my design but through just allowing yourself to enter this repetitive almost breathing motion of taking a ball of clay and using the space between your hands as a kind of mould, a kind of womb out of which the form arises. Each person is communicating a unique self in the way they walk, the way they write their name, the way they speak. I do fundamentally believe that each of us is an artist, is a creative person and the project that we are making is the self: the shape of our lives. This work and process is a way of expressing that.

And what happens when people do this?

I think you become a tribe. If you weren't beforehand, you become a tribe through the process of making it. People are always amazed that they can do this extraordinary thing of making an object that in some way is part of them and part of their bodies and they put it out there, and it has a life of its own and it makes demands of you. I think that's what was extraordinary about *Field*. That's certainly what happened when we made it at St Helen's, filling up this 1960s school. First of all we filled the gym, then we filled the science block and we ended up in the schoolrooms, filling every available surface, the floor and all the tabletops with this growing crowd. People couldn't believe the energy of this battery of gazes that was looking back at them because each of the figures has two little eyes that look up and forward, eagerly awaiting something or other.

Can you not see that this is your congregation?

The interesting thing is that each person who made part of it became the work's first audience and was aware of the power of the pieces. I think the whole point about *Field* is that it's saying, 'We are no longer God's children; we are the makers of the world; we are the inheritors of this earth; and out of it we make a world.' And in some senses, each of us carries a responsibility for that.

Does it express a faith in man? Do you have faith in the future, or do you feel it's an arid desert?

I think *Field* combines all sorts of fears with a great deal of faith. It talks about over-population and lots of our worries about what we're doing to the planet. But I think it also is life-enhancing or life-empowering in so far as it puts you in the position of being the mediator between, as it were, the spirit of the ancestors and the spirit of the unborn. That we are this living layer of human consciousness that is in some senses the seeds of the future.

And is the world good?

I think the world is a place of transformation in which the forces of good and evil are ever waging a constant battle. I am not sure that I believe in an evolution from bad to good. I think that what we have to do is remain vigilant and keep in some sense our faith that human consciousness is the agency by which balance can be maintained in the world.

2

JAMES LOVELOCK

'The odds are quite high that we'll revert back to being tribal carnivores'

James Lovelock is a uniquely innovative scientist. In the 1970s he developed the Gaia Theory, a theory that sees the earth as though it were a living organism. This notion has been hailed as the most original way of looking at the planet since Darwin, and has been adopted – or adapted – to serve the ideas of New Agers, some of whom look upon Gaia as a new sort of religion. To establish exactly where his theory fits within scientific thought, I asked him about the moment in 1965 when it first occurred to him.

Well, I'd been working at the Jet Propulsion Labs in California, on the problem of how do we find life on Mars. It's still a problem and NASA's still trying to do it. But that was about the time they started. And I had the view that you could tell if there's life on a planet, just by looking at the whole planet – not by going and grubbing around on the surface looking for bugs or giraffes or something.

I was in a small office room with Carl Sagan the astronomer, a friend of mine Diane Hitchcock, who is a philosopher, and an astronomer, Lou Caplan. And an astronomer had just brought in the analyses of the atmospheres of Mars and Venus. My theory was that if those planets had atmospheres that are chemical equilibrium unreactive – then they'd be dead planets. And sure enough they were. And this suddenly made me think about the earth. The air we breathe is extraordinary. It's a mixture of reactive gases. There's methane, natural gas, mixed with oxygen. If the concentrations were different it would be combustible or explosive. It suddenly came into my mind 'This can't be by accident. For such an unstable atmosphere to stay stable for millions of years is quite remarkable. Something's going on, something must be regulating it. What can it be, other than life at the surface?'

What was conducive to that insight entering your mind at that particular moment? Were you very relaxed or very excited?

No, it was much more continually thinking about this problem – how do you find life on Mars or somewhere else by analysing the atmosphere of the planet? And all sorts of thoughts and information had got stacked away at the back of my mind. And I think suddenly it all came together at that moment, when they told me about Mars and Venus.

Would you explain what Gaia Theory is?

I see it as a new theory of evolution. The evolution of the earth itself. It builds on Darwin's great theory of the evolution of the living organisms by natural selection, but it brings the evolution of the air, the oceans and the rocks in with Darwin's evolution. So that they're not two separate processes taught in two separate buildings in the university – they're one, great system. And as a consequence of life and its environment evolving tightly coupled together, the remarkable and wonderful process of self-regulation emerges from this joint system.

And it doesn't contradict Darwinism?

In no way does it contradict Darwinism.

What was your perception of the world around you as a child?

I was brought up by my grandmother, because my mother was very much an early feminist, and she wanted to lead a life of her own unfettered by children. And she was running with my father a shop in Brixton. And they didn't want a young baby running around. So my grandmother brought me up. And it was a very loving atmosphere. Nobody in the family – grandparents or parents – was formally religious. But in those days the whole world was marinated with religion. You couldn't escape it. It was everywhere. And not only religion, but interestingly people were very superstitious in those days. Everybody touched wood, threw salt over their shoulder. In fact I was so affected by it, that it took a conscious act in my twenties to stop doing it. I thought 'I can't go on doing this – I'm a scientist. It's absolute nonsense!'

What started you off on your scientific life?

I think my father set me on the right steps in two ways. When I was only four years old, he gave me a box of tricks which was full of wires and batteries and bells and things, said 'Join that up, you'll have a lot of fun with it', which I did. It was the best Christmas present I had. And I remember getting very puzzled about 'Why did you need two wires to send electricity along, whereas if you were sending gas and water, a single pipe would do?' So I started questioning people about this – even the postman. And nobody could answer it. And I thought 'Well if you're going to ask questions like that, you'll have to start to find out for yourself somehow.'

So you were a practical, applied maker of things?

Exactly, and always have been – still am.

To all matters you study you bring a highly individual system of analysis. Was that part of your education?

No, no. It just happened. The other way my father helped, he had an extraordinary childhood himself – extreme poverty – his father died when they were young and there were 13 children. And when he was 14, as part of his job as elder child, looking after the family, he was caught poaching by a local gamekeeper, and sent to Reading jail for six months' hard labour. The things that happened in those days! But having been an apprentice poacher so to speak, he knew all about wildlife and the countryside. It was an enlightenment just to go for country walks with him. So there was that side of science coming in also.

Also there was an impulse to socialist thinking – a background of sympathy with socialist ideals, which has stayed with you.

My mother was as socialist as you could get. I mean she wouldn't even believe that Stalin committed those awful crimes. She thought it was propaganda. She firmly believed to her dying day that there was no truth in it at all, that he couldn't possibly have done that. That was faith for you!

When it came to World War II, you were a conscientious objector. That seems quite unusual for World War II, because in political terms it was seen as an absolutely just war. What made you a conscientious objector?

Oh, I must disagree with you there. If you go back to the 1930s, '38, an awful lot of people were pacifist. They felt that war was so bad that it couldn't possibly be a solution – there must be another solution.

Did they make it hard for you to get exemption from military service?

No, that was what's so troubling. I thought that being a conscientious objector was a noble thing to do. I'd been brought up in the tradition of a group of Quakers who had been conscientious objectors in World War I and had had a very hard time indeed. And I was expecting to go to prison, to follow in my father's footsteps. And I expected the tribunal to be exceedingly difficult, and to have a rough time. Instead of which, I stood before three very civilised judges, who were most understanding and helpful, and said 'Yes, well, we leave it to your conscience to do what you think is right, and give you an unconditional exemption.' I couldn't believe it at the time. I felt 'This is not what I'd expected at all.'

There came a moment, when you asked for that exemption to be lifted.

About two years later, and after the Blitz, when things were getting really rough, I felt it wasn't possible for me to feel at ease in a society where everybody was pulling their weight, where the food I ate was brought by brave merchant seamen, who often died across the sea. You just couldn't any longer, so I gave up.

As time went by, you became an inventor, and invented something called the Electron Capture Detector. Can you explain it?

It's a small, electronic device. I like to think of it as just a test tube full of electrons. Its remarkable property is that it detects only nasty things – poisons, carcinogens, pesticides and chloro-fluorocarbons – things like that. It was the first time that chemists had available something that would pick up pesticides in food-stuffs, chloro-fluorocarbons in the atmosphere and so on. It has been very valuable for environmental needs.

Why was this such a major breakthrough?

The whole environment was at risk of being poisoned. They were using pesticides ad lib, in a rather uncontrolled manner. Rachel Carson's book *Silent Spring* raised the alarm. I gave her the back-up scientifically. Anybody who doubted what she was saying could have the evidence from my apparatus. It made clear there really was a serious problem.

You went to America, and you've said that 'Chance favoured me with a view of the earth from space', that moved you towards your theory. What was that moment? What was that chance?

It was this business of looking at planets like Mars, from the outside. Nobody before NASA came along had had a chance to look at the earth from outside. Everyone remembers those extraordinary photographs that the astronauts first showed of the earth as that gorgeous sphere. It's become almost banal now and an icon advertising soap or something. But when it first appeared it was enthralling, and to me it still is. But that wasn't the only way you could see the earth from outside. You could see it with instruments that NASA sent up, and look at the atmosphere from outside and see in it all sorts of things. The earth had never been looked at that way before.

You use the word 'gorgeous' – it's a subjective word. So did you feel engaged with the earth on that level?

Very much so. And if you talk to quite a few astronauts, all of them that have been outside and looked back at the earth, get that same feeling. That's home – it isn't the street or the town or the country – that's home. You know … They send messages saying 'It is *so* beautiful.'

This quality of beauty is not a scientific measure but it helped you evolve something that was quite scientific: the Gaia Theory. Explain the use of the phrase 'The earth is a living organism'. You used it as a metaphor to help us understand, but it has led to misunderstanding.

And a lot of criticism. You mentioned that as a scientist I was used to making my own instruments. And when you make instruments, you begin to understand what engineers call 'fed back systems' – control systems. Things that have negative and positive feedback, and keep themselves steady. Even like the refrigerator in your home. And when you understand that, and you think about something like the earth, and discover that it's self-regulating, just like the refrigerator is in your home, you begin to think 'Well it's behaving like a living organism.' Each one of us holds our temperature reasonably constant. It never varies much more than five degrees – at the lowest 35, at the maximum 40 – but it nearly always sits within there. Our extremities can go right the way down nearly to freezing and get even hotter when we put our hands in hot water. And the earth's just like that – it holds its temperature between about 10 and 15 Celsius – within the same five degrees, and always has done. That makes it unique in the solar system. And the means by which it does that I have called 'Gaia'.

Where did the name 'Gaia' come from?

Shortly after the idea came into my mind, I discussed it with a neighbour of mine in the village I lived in then, the great novelist William Golding. I didn't know he was a great novelist then – he was just another chap in the village who knew all about physics, because he'd been trained in physics at university. We were walking to the post office one day, and I started telling him about my idea about how the earth self-regulates and he got very interested, and we walked way beyond the post office and then turned around and came back. And on the way back he said 'Well you know, I think if you've got a big idea like that, you'd better give it a proper name, and I suggest Gaia.' And we walked on for at least ten minutes in total misunderstanding. I thought he meant 'G-Y-R-E' – one of those great whirls in the ocean – not 'G-A-I-A'. And then we resolved it. He said 'No, no, no, no I mean "Gaia" – the Greek goddess of the earth.'

Do you think the choice of Gaia, a lyrical sound … has made some people think it was less scientific than in fact it is?

I'm not sure about that. I think scientists were made to think that by the biologists who saw it as a threat to Darwin. They were quite wrong of course, but they saw it that way, which was understandable. And they were very touchy about any threat to Darwin, and the name Gaia was an easy target. 'Fancy naming a theory after a Greek goddess!' Well they forgot, of course, that geography and geology are named after exactly the same goddess.

Now the earth is not 'living' in the sense that we're living. It doesn't have motive, it doesn't have intention, but nonetheless, it behaves as though it did, and as though its destiny was to perpetuate itself.

That's right. As long as you keep in mind that the refrigerator in your kitchen has in a sense a goal. You set the temperature – whatever it is – that it should be at, with a little dial in the inside. And if your kitchen gets warmer it will automatically adjust the power it takes, to keep the temperature at exactly that. And if it gets very cold in the kitchen, it'll use less – it's automatic, self-regulating. That's what the earth is.

How does Gaia interact with humanity?

We are part of it. We are part of it in two ways. In one way, we're just another animal species – we're recycling the oxygen that the trees produce, eating plants and animals so as to recycle the carbon dioxide – we're just part of the whole system as an animal, a top predator. But as an intelligent species, we're interfering with the whole system and making changes. Our reaction roughly is that if we make changes to the earth that are favourable, that will allow us to leave more progeny, then by Darwin's rules, we'll succeed. We'll be a successful species. If on the other hand we affect the atmosphere and the oceans and soil of the earth in a way that lessens our chances to leave progeny, then we'll go extinct, as many organisms have gone extinct in the past.

And so going extinct would be part of the earth's behaviour?

Automatic behaviour. And the earth would go on, whatever we do. We're feeble, compared with it – nothing we can do is going to kill it off. But what we can do is damage civilisation.

What about man as a spiritual being? Because you have said that 'For me, Gaia is a religious, as well as a scientific concept.'

Yes, I said that a long time ago. I'd be a bit more cautious now. But I stick by what I said. Because it's largely a matter of semantics and understanding words. I think everyone has a need to have something to respect and to worship. And I think one of the best candidates for that is the earth itself, because it's tangible. We live on it, we are part of it. It has ethical associations, does Gaia Theory. The earth is something to which we are accountable. If we do right by the earth, then we will benefit. If we do wrong, we'll be punished – and that has ethical, religious connotations to it.

What about belief in God? We can't worship the earth, can we?

I don't see why we shouldn't. Some people do. And many ancient people did. I can see no reason why worship shouldn't operate in that direction. I don't know anything about God. I'm an agnostic – I'm not an atheist – I think that's much too strong a position. It's too certain. It's says 'I know that science tells me there is no God.' Well science tells nothing of the kind. It just says there's no evidence and I go along with that. I just don't know whether there's a God or not a God.

When you were developing the Gaia Theory and people were being very snooty about it in many quarters, you offered them a description which has been called 'daisy world' as a demonstration of it. Can you summarise that for me?

Well, first of all among the scientific community Richard Dawkins was a really good critic and any theory needs good critics. I'm jolly grateful to him, because he pointed out that the Gaia hypothesis was plain wrong from a biological point of view. We said life or the biosphere regulates the atmosphere, the oceans, and so on, so as to keep the earth habitable. He said 'That's impossible – there's no way for organisms to regulate anything beyond their own bodies. They couldn't possibly evolve so as to regulate the earth.' And after a couple of years thinking I realised he was right, we were wrong. And then I thought 'But I know it self-regulates. I know it's a system – so how does it do it – what's happening?' And it suddenly dawned on me, maybe it's the whole system – that's to say the environment and life together, unified, that's doing the self-regulating – not life. And so I made a model – that's the thing scientists do – to try and demonstrate this. And it was a very simple model. I made a simple world which rotated around a sun just like the earth. And there were just two species on it that I was going to consider – dark and light coloured daisies. And there was only one variable I was going to look at – that was temperature. Could the Darwinian evolution and those two daisy species competing with one another regulate the temperature of the planet at the right temperature for daisy growth and keep it stable during the course of a change of output of heat from the sun that was warming it. And when I made the model, to my delight, it regulated near perfectly at exactly the best temperature for daisy growth.

And what did your critics have to say?

Oh, they all grumbled about it like mad. The editor of *Nature* recently had an editorial, in which he stated 'Probably no model has so irritated earth and life sciences in the twentieth century as did simple model daisy world.' And it's true – they hated it.

Have you ever doubted the soundness of your theory?

Yes – all the time. Because I was perhaps over-confident when the Gaia hypothesis appeared, that life regulates the system. And it was only when a good critic like Richard Dawkins came along that I realised I was wrong. And all science does that – that's what's wonderful about science. We're never certain about anything.

Let's go into more detail about the ethical consequences of this theory. Because strangely enough, you are not always at one with the environmentalists today. You have been pro-nuclear energy, for example. Why do you not chime in with them?

34

I think it's fairly simple. If you look at the Green movement, it mostly grew up from groups like CND. They were very political, left-wing political mostly. And they had a very right cause – that was during the Cold War – they didn't want a nuclear Armageddon and they were right to march against it. But the problem with the Green movement as I see it is they're mainly concerned with what I would call 'people problems'. They worry about nuclear radiation, about pesticides, about poisons and so on. But they worried far less about damage to the earth. It is only recently that the Green movement has begun to take aboard the greenhouse problem. As an Earth Scientist, I see it from almost the opposite viewpoint. It's the earth's problems that are really crucial not only for the earth, but for people. I mean if pesticides were unregulated, if we all had nuclear power stations to the extent that the French do, everywhere in the world, I think that'd be a minor problem compared with the global greenhouse. And not only just that, but the need to farm so much of the earth to feed people is beginning to interfere with the natural ecosystems that do the regulation. So it's not just a matter of poisoning the atmosphere. It's also a matter of not taking everything from the earth, because then there'll be nothing left to take care of us.

Some New Agers have taken on Gaia – they like the name – it feels like a religion. Do you feel that they have misused the Gaia Theory?

To quite an extent, yes. They don't say 'The earth behaves as if it were alive.' They say 'The earth's alive! Because she will do this and that…' And this not only upsets scientists, but it leads them up wrong tracks, I never meant that at all.

Are we going to survive? Are we a doomed species by our own hand?

I think humans are exceedingly tough. They're one of the

toughest species on earth. I think even if there was a major meteoric hit, there would be humans surviving somewhere, on a small farm in New Zealand or something. And we would build back again. And so I'm not worried about the human species *per se*. I think we've got a long time to go. What I'm worried about mainly is civilisation. That's much more fragile.

But won't Gaia Theory somehow be taking care of that?

I don't think so. It'll be taking care of the planet, sure. But it won't be taking care of us. We're the irritant. And the changes we induce may make it increasingly more uncomfortable for civilisation. You have to look at it like this. Gaia's very good at looking after the big jobs. If there's a major impact, she'll see that life goes on and that the earth self-regulates and keeps a fit place, a habitat for life. But the fine tuning, she's not so hot at. And if we mess about with the environment, what we're most likely to do is to make the whole world very uncomfortable for humans and for animals that go along with us.

So do you believe we're faced with a real possibility of a Dark Age?

I feel very much that habitat destruction, the taking away of the natural ecosystems that regulate the world both on the land and in the sea, and adding greenhouse gases to the atmosphere threaten us with a new Dark Age where there will be no civilisation. Humans will be tough enough to survive, but it won't be a very nice world for quite a while The odds are quite high that we'll revert back to what we are, tribal carnivores.

What's the future of Gaia itself?

The planet itself is quite old. It's existed with life on it for four billion years, that's about Gaia's age. But we're pretty certain that she doesn't have more than about one billion to go.

So in human terms, four-fifths of her life has gone, and if she was good for a hundred, she must be about eighty. In other words, she's about my age, and I think that's an age where folk should be treated with care and respect.

3

TERRY EAGLETON

'A synthesis of Christianity and Marxism makes a lot of intellectual sense'

Terry Eagleton is Britain's foremost Marxist literary critic, whose teaching and writing about literary theory have dominated several decades of British cultural life. After studying at Cambridge with Raymond Williams, he took up a teaching post at Oxford where he remained for 30 years. In 1991 he was made Warton Professor of English there. In 2001 he became Professor of Cultural Theory and John Rylands Fellow at Manchester University – a post created for him. His book Criticism and Ideology *in 1976 made his reputation; then in 1983 his* Literary Theory – an Introduction *put him on the world stage. His most recent work,* After Theory, *was published in 2004. He has written a play,* Saint Oscar, *a novel,* Saints and Scholars, *a film,* Wittgenstein, *with Derek Jarman, and an autobiography* The Gatekeeper, *the title of which refers to his Catholic childhood.*

As a small boy I served mass in a rather spooky Carmelite convent of enclosed Carmelite nuns who were very poor, and led a very hard life, and knew nothing about what was going on in the world. One of my jobs was to do a few chores around the place and this included ushering in the parents of a nun who was just about to be taken into the convent, knowing that they would never see her again, because she would be totally enclosed for the rest of her life. Being the 'gatekeeper' as it were, while this happened. So I suppose this was a traumatic enough memory to finally end up as a book title.

Were you aware of grief and sacrifice and pain?

I knew what was going on enough at that age, and I also knew the nuns seemed very happy. They led the most atrociously hard life. I think they slept on planks, and they ate very little, and really knew nothing of what was going on in the outside world. I suppose that first planted in me the thought of sacrifice and what it was, which later was to emerge in a more political form. But that's probably where it began.

You speak of yourself as a 'cradle Catholic', and its two prevailing legacies for you are your sense of dogma, and also your sense of authority. Both were later to apply to your Marxism. But what did dogma and authority in the Catholic Church mean to the learning boy?

A polite way of describing the move I've made from Catholicism to Marxism is to go from one dogmatic, authoritarian system to another. Or as I sometimes say, you don't have to go through liberalism. You can take a short cut and jump from one to the other.

Dogma actually means simply 'things taught'. It doesn't necessarily have this autocratic or closed-minded emphasis. Though of course there's a lot of that around in the Catholic Church. It always seems to me a mistake to be against authority as such. It seems to me it all depends on what kind of authority and for what reasons. I think I grew up in an extremely autocratic, closed-minded and sectarian church. And a church that, because of that, has blighted the lives of millions of people. But I was also aware that there were good meanings of belief and doctrine and authority, and also of community. In a rather grotesquely parodic kind of way this claustrophobic, convent-like world also had a deep belief in the value of community. If you were born a working-class Catholic in Britain, as I was, you don't grow up into a liberal, individualist tradition. And missing out on that in one sense is very damaging but it also puts you in touch with certain forms of solidarity and sharing and community that's valuable.

So everyone you knew as a child, believed in the Immaculate Conception, the Resurrection of the Body, the Salvation?

Well of course, those all paled into insignificance beside the infallibility of the Pope. I mean you could disbelieve the others, as long as you believed in the Pope. Except there is a question there, isn't there, about what belief meant? They did sign on for those articles of faith, but belief in a way didn't come into it. I mean belief implies some kind of personal commitment.

This was simply a 'given'?

This was a 'given'. And that wasn't just the case for us little lay people – it was the case for the clergy, it was the case for the bishops. I remember the Archbishop of Westminster at the time, saying that he'd never had a single doubt in his life about his faith. And I believed him, because I knew what he meant. It wasn't the kind of thing you would doubt.

It wasn't an arena in which you exercised any kind of curiosity?

It wasn't recommended, I think. But it was simply a system you were given, and you grew up with. It took me a long time to realise that faith is a kind of commitment you just find you can't walk away from, however hard you try. And you don't really have that kind of choice about it.

So the De la Salle brothers at the grammar school you attended, were simply part of this belief system, too?

They were. They were mainly Irish lads who'd made it 'out of the bog' by becoming brothers. They didn't necessarily want to be, but it was a way out. And they'd come, as they would've seen it, on the 'missions' to England. They spoke about it as the 'missions'. I'd like to able to indulge in a little lurid melodrama in a James Joyce way, and say that they were extremely bullying and brutal and abusive. Actually they weren't. They were on the whole not terribly bright, but decent guys, whose job was (a) to knock this sort of stuff into us, and (b) more importantly, to get us into the English social system. To get us out of the ghetto into the English system.

Did this belief system where you found yourself – did it involve personal feelings of love, of awe, of fear?

No, absolutely not. And that is indeed what's so ludicrous about it. I mean to call this belief, it's like calling having measles belief. Faith was absolutely nothing personal. Or to do with love, or even to do with people.

Behaviour?

Yes behaviour, conduct – sure. But not conduct that had much to do with the idea of love, or the idea of mercy or forgiveness. One believed all these things in an abstract kind of way.

You speak about the Church as being a 'given' rather than a belief. What about being working class, was that 'given'?

Well it was a 'given'. That's why one of the most native pastimes in Ireland was trying to get out of the place. I remember the day when my primary school headmaster at a very rough school told me I'd passed the Eleven-Plus. And I remember my delight, and I also remember knowing what it meant. It meant 'out', and, and I knew what the consequences were if I hadn't got out.

Now your father was bright, and he could have achieved, but didn't and it wasn't his fault. And he went into a silent world of acceptance of his own life.

Yes. I'm not sure it was acceptance. I would guess there was perhaps a very deep, silent rejection going on there but one that he didn't have the words for. He certainly regarded himself politically as a Socialist, which was an influence upon me. And he, also, connected that with his faith.

And what influence do you think he had on you?

Hard to say. Here's somebody who's feeding into you and symbolising that which you have to get away from. And that's a hellishly difficult situation. We drifted out of touch for a while as I became an adolescent, partly because he was a very practical man, which I'm not, and he didn't really understand an interest in the arts.

So you go to Trinity College, Cambridge: the toff's college. What was that like?

At the time it felt like sheer hell. I spent most of my time in Cambridge trying to get out, and I was just about to get out after I'd graduated when I bumped into Raymond Williams, my great mentor and friend. And it was he who really kept me there. And there was that curious sense that I was doing all this partly for my father, and for my family. And yet of course, it meant also breaking with him and to some degree, breaking politically from what he stood for. So it was very painful.

And the news of his death was given to you just as you were taking your exams to go to Cambridge.

In those days you had to go down rather intimidatingly to Cambridge, to take all of these papers – and have an interview with your prospective tutor. And my interview consisted in my tutor telling me that my father had died. He, poor man, did it very badly. How would you do that thing well you might ask?! I think he was more upset at that very moment than I was. I knew my father was dying, because he was dying when I left home. But it sort of brought to a head all of the symbolic contradictions in the situation, I suppose.

And did you feel that the legacy of his death was that you would live out perhaps, on his behalf, the things he might've been capable of himself?

I saw my work as giving him a tongue, because it was his silence which struck me most forcibly – a very resonant silence. But at the same time, I gave him and what he stood for a tongue in a language that he didn't speak. So across the generations there remained that filament, that affiliation of political faith I think, that kept us together.

While at Cambridge you remained very much a Catholic student. You founded the magazine SLANT *which took a liberal view of Catholicism, and you came under the influence of the Dominican Laurence Bright. By now you're very conscious of what belief is, and that belief can be challenged. So what was going on?*

What was going on was that just at the moment when any

decent, civilised human being would've left the Church, the Vatican Council broke out all over the place. Lots of exciting things were happening in the Church. People like Laurence Bright and Herbert McCabe, a great friend of mine, a theologian, were part of that. And now, you could reject the Catholicism that I was brought up with very easily. But I'd now encountered, somewhat to my dismay, a version of the Gospel, which wasn't easy to reject, because it spoke very deeply to my political and moral and cultural interests.

And what happened to all your beliefs in Vatican II and the liberalisation of the Church?

Well in a word, it didn't work, I think. In some ways Vatican II filtered into the whole Christian culture. In other ways it just didn't achieve what it wanted to. The Christian left movement split up for all kinds of reasons, and we were all rather left out in the cold in a very different kind of society – basically in Thatcher's Britain. Don't forget that this period at Cambridge, and the Catholic left and the Vatican Council had all really coincided with '68 and the youth student movement. So that was when we felt things were moving for us, and it was very hard to reinvent that moment later.

We were not at the wrong time, we were at the wrong place. A lot of what we were arguing about the radical nature of the Christian Gospel actually made a lot of sense, and was being lived out in places like Latin America. Or indeed, and to some extent, across the water in Ireland, as the Troubles were beginning. There you didn't have to argue for a connection between political faith and religious faith – it was sort of given. And partly because of that, I always retained some relationship to theology. Because theology for me certainly meant something that was revolutionary. Still does in fact, insofar as I talk about it. It meant something that was on the side of the dispossessed rather than on the side of the rulers.

Spell out for me the move that you are beginning to make as you see that Vatican II isn't really working. It's a cliché to say you moved from one ideology to another. But how did it work?

I suppose at the time we were trying out some sort of synthesis of Christianity and Marxism, which I think makes a lot of intellectual sense. It was just all rather a lot of belief to stagger around with. It belonged to a very particular historical moment, when it looked on the one hand as though the Church was moving forward, and on the other hand, there was a wider political context to make sense of that. Both of those things finally dissipated, so most of us in the Christian left moved off into various forms of secular politics. And I got interested in Marxism and the work of Raymond Williams, and carried that on. But as I say, it was a rather particular, unique moment that had vanished. It wasn't to be recovered.

What were the tenets of Marxism that commanded your allegiance?

It was for me very much a secular equivalent, or version of what I saw as the revolutionary nature of the Gospel. I mean if you look at the Book of Isaiah, it wouldn't be everybody's candidate for a revolutionary document, but it certainly is. It's pretty obvious from the Book of Isaiah, indeed from the Old Testament in general, that this Yahweh is the God of the dispossessed, and as Isaiah says 'You'll know who he is when you see the hungry being filled with good things and the rich being sent empty away.' The God of the Book of Isaiah is extremely infuriated by religion. He keeps telling the Jews that their incense stinks in his nostrils and why don't they stop all this liturgy and start taking care of the widows and the orphans and the immigrants. That was the kind of Gospel that made sense to me as a Marxist. One didn't really have to argue the connections. The whole thing had been turned into an idolatrous scandal by the Church, and the Christian Gospel then, as now, is largely propaganda for the rich and powerful of the world. And if we couldn't break that within the Church, then I guess the idea was we moved outside it, into various kinds of organisation.

But Marxism wasn't social welfare – it was about world revolution.
Well I think Yahweh was about world revolution as well! I don't think he was terribly interested in health visitors.

Marxism was getting its break in the early '70s, which was probably when the hopes of the left peaked in Britain. You were out on the streets, distributing the newspaper of whichever sect it was you belonged to at the time. Did you feel very much part of the army moving forward?
I think yes. I think that's the difference between the left now and then. It wasn't that at that time everybody was on the left, or everybody was a Marxist – it was that there was a certain kind of culture within which those beliefs made sense. You didn't have to subscribe to them necessarily, but they made a kind of sense. I think that's what's changed. I mean my beliefs haven't changed as far as that goes. I suppose people some-times criticise me for jumping on the post-structuralist bandwagon and then some other bandwagon. I think the genuine criticism of my work is I've been far too consistent. I mean I pretty well believe now what I believed then.

The older tradition of literary criticism – taught by dons like F.R. Leavis – was that the canon of great literature carried the moral message for the culture. Your teaching and those who came with you set that aside in the interests of a new way of expressing the purpose of literature and its moral role. What were the parameters of the new idea?

Well I think it may be a little too quick to say we were setting aside the whole of the moral emphasis of literature in the sense of concern with quality of life, quality of relationship. The new theory really wanted to put that in a broader historical, cultural, political context. So I don't see it as throwing out the moral by any means. I see it as actually contextualising it in a richer way.

It was a question of overcoming that fatal division whereby the moral is somehow confined to either the bedroom or the kitchen, or at least the private realm, and politics is left to take care of the public one. That means that one gets some very unhappy kitchens and bedrooms, and one gets some very immoral public politics.

At Oxford, where you were English tutor at Wadham College you helped bring into the syllabus the work of women writers, black writers, working-class writers. And that was presumably an attempt to shift this whole moral perspective that we're speaking of.

Oxford's a very difficult place to do that in, and I was part of a group who did that over a number of years. The Humanities of course has been changing all over the world and Oxford stood out against it for a long time. But eventually even Oxford has fallen in that respect.

There were critics who claimed you were disenfranchising the author, and the authenticity of the authorial experience. Now you're an author yourself, presumably you have second thoughts about that?

I think that was always a bit of a caricature actually. There's a French critic and poet who said that 'there are more things involved in the creation of a work of art than the author', and that's all we were saying. Of course authors are important, but they're one element. And as authors well know, they're not in total control or mastery of what they're doing. There are many other factors … unconscious, historical, ideological, literary, stylistic – that enter into that very bizarre act of creation. So I think we were not denying the authors' right in their works, we were saying 'Look, a too rigidly author-centred idea of literature is far too narrow – it leaves out far too much.'

We've spoken without defining it, about the difficulty of defining morality. What are the precepts that you regard as important in terms of individual behaviour?

Well, my friend the theologian Herbert McCabe – a Dominican theologian – summarised the morality of the New Testament in one rather arresting sentence. He said that what the New Testament teaches is that 'If you don't love, you're dead, and if you do, they'll kill you.' One has to try and codify that, in a sense one has to say 'Well what does that mean? What counts as love and what counts as life?' I think the language of morality is trying to specify more concretely what that is. Extraordinarily, people sometimes think that it's just some sort of consolation. I don't find it much consolation that you might be killed. So I think that morality has to start from there, and then progressively specify what that would mean in particular situations.

We've spoken about the theory of being a writer, and the theory of morality. But you have been a writer yourself. You've written Saints and Sinners, *which was a novel about Wittgenstein, and you've written a play* Saint Oscar, *which is about Oscar Wilde. The word 'saint' crops up in many of these titles and I can't think that's an accident.*

No, I'm sure it isn't, although I also wrote a film script about Wittgenstein. It wasn't actually called *'St Wittgenstein'*, but it could've been. I also, for some deep reason I entirely fail to understand, tend to write about rather austere martyr-like figures. Which is not the way I feel about myself particularly. I'm interested in the idea of sacrifice in some sense other than the drearily oppressive notion of sacrifice that is so common morally today.

Is this now a synthesis of your Catholicism and your Marxism, the fact that sacrifice is something that is applicable in both ideologies?

Yes, and I think there's a bit of Freud in there as well if one were to pursue it further. Martyrs are not people who want to die. Martyrs give up what they think is most precious – their life. Martyrs are not the same as suicides. Somebody who commits suicide does so because their life has become a burden to them – intolerable. Martyrs properly seen, are dying very reluctantly, giving up the thing they regard as the most valuable, for the sake of others.

It seems to me you're holding on to these two traditions in your life. You're not grasping them in any kind of fanatical sense. But you are holding them and letting them nourish your ongoing evolution.

Yes, and that goes back to what I said right at the beginning … belief is something that grips you, rather than that you choose. I mean that utterly mistaken idea of belief that it's: 'Well here are the various hats, Christian, existentialist, Buddhist – now which one shall I wear today?' I suppose because I'm a bit more confident intellectually than I used to be, and because I'm a lot older, than when I started out, I'm now able in a sense to go with what I feel. And that's not to deny that there must've been a lot of intellectual analysis there. But it's to trust that in some way.

But does it sit comfortably with you, getting older and moving towards the end of your life? Do you feel comfortable with what may happen, or not, when you die?

I never particularly felt very comfortable about dying. But I do I think that I've been able to retain something of my past, not in the same form. But I've been able to make something out of it. I've been able to make something positive out of what in some respects was a pretty painful and a rather isolated and alienating kind of experience. I'm always a great believer in trying to retrieve or rescue something and make a good use out of it, even if it seems superficially unpropitious for that use. And I believe I've done that.

4

KAREN ARMSTRONG

'Follow the Bliss'

At the age of 17 Karen Armstrong entered the Society of the Holy Child Jesus. Seven years later she left the Order: her vocation to be a nun having ended in failure. In her book Through the Narrow Gate *– published in 1981 – she explained why. Then in its sequel,* The Spiral Staircase: my Climb out of Darkness, *she offered new insights into her religious journey. After her convent years she became an academic researching and writing books about the world's religions. They include* A History of God, The Battle for God: A History of Fundamentalism, Islam: A Short History *and* Buddha. *Since 9/11 she has been much in demand as a lecturer, on both sides of the Atlantic. But it is her identity as an ex-nun that most fascinates her British readers.*

It's the 'ex' that I object to, rather than the nun part of it, because in some strange turn-around, I've remained quite nun-like in many ways. I've never married, I live alone and I spend my days writing, thinking, talking about God and spirituality, so I sometimes think that when I decided to enter a convent all those years ago as a young and very ignorant teenager, I was having a stab perhaps, at the kind of life I've got now but which wasn't available to me at that time.

Let's examine how you got there. Your father was a convert Roman Catholic....

Yes, but my parents weren't religious people, particularly. We went along to mass on Sunday mornings – often went as early as possible to get it all over and out of the way – and then rushed home and enjoyed the rest of the day. We weren't a devout family and my parents, poor things, were horrified when I decided that I wanted to be a nun.

Was it an act of rebellion?

A bit, in a way. There was part of me that felt ill at ease in the kind of late '50s, very early '60s society, that was very family-based and I lived in Birmingham, which was a very materialistic part of the country, where money was king and I, in my idealistic teenage way, didn't like that. I wanted to find God, I had very vague ideas what this meant but I thought I would immediately become wise, serene, Buddha-like, and perhaps, lose all this adolescent confusion that so plagues a 17-year-old. It didn't happen.

When you wrote your book you said you had strong religious beliefs as a child but little faith in God. Can you enlarge on the distinction?

Well, yes, in the Western world since the eighteenth century, we've tended to equate faith with believing things, with accepting certain ideas, doctrines or propositions about God, heaven, and the afterlife. But that's a very peculiar development in the history of religion. Other religious traditions – I'm thinking of Judaism, Islam, Buddhism – don't place any much credence on belief. Basically you can believe what you want, it's not important, what is important is doing things, living in a certain way – uniformity of practice very often, rather than uniformity of belief. But we in the West have gone in for believing things and when I was in my convent, I had strong beliefs about the existence of God, the nature of Jesus Christ and redemption but I cannot say that that gave me any great faith that life had ultimate meaning and value. The word faith implies that in a sense despite all the depressing evidence to the contrary, life does have some ultimate meaning.

And you never found that, even in the convent?

The God I thought I believed in, was a very harsh taskmaster, a cosmic Big Brother, endlessly looking down, marking up my every fault, never satisfied with what I did. I was never able to please him and indeed, never able to get in contact with him. I expected to have all kinds of wonderful spiritual experiences but the heavens remained obstinately closed. When I eventually lost my belief in this God, life became a whole lot better.

But wasn't prayer meaningful to you at that time?

I was absolutely hopeless at prayer. I could not meditate at all. Every morning we'd go into the chapel at six o' clock and meditate until seven and I could not keep my mind on this for more than two minutes at a time. Now I have no problem with concentration normally. I can sit over my books at my desk for hours and not notice the time going by. But it was the wrong kind of prayer for me. Plus it was a bad time to become a nun – it was just before the changes wrought by the Second Vatican Council and I was one of the last people to go through a system that was very flawed, that was endlessly driving into us a sense of our faults and failings and I think, we were so inured and embedded in egotistic anxiety about our own performance, we couldn't possibly have had a religious experience.

Did you find love there?

No, it was a very cold environment. We weren't allowed for example, to have friends. We were supposed, in those days, to give all our love to God, so particular friendship, in most religious communities, was frowned upon. We were never allowed to speak in twos, always had to wait 'til a third person came along and indeed, most of our days were passed in silence. So it combined religious devotion with the English stiff upper lip and reserve and so it was a fairly lethal mixture. It was this cold-heartedness that eventually I rebelled against. I said that this had nothing whatever to do with the Gospels, where you have a very hands-on, engaged Jesus going out, loving people and very much involved with them, and where love and concern for the neighbour and affection for the neighbour is at the heart of piety. I've come to believe that compassion, love, feeling with people, is at the heart of the religious life.

The Mother Superior said to you at one point, that brain work distracted the mind, so that even thinking was considered as getting in the way of God.

Yes, and this I think was a hangover from the Victorian period, where women were not supposed to be great brains. In fact, women weren't supposed to have brains much at all. It was thought until relatively recently that our brains were so fragile that they would crumble under the impact of real strenuous thinking. So most of the time I spent sewing, scrubbing floors and even made a disastrous foray into cooking.

Did it make you feel guilty?

Just despairing and hopeless, and I think what I felt most guilty about was that I was continually in tears and I'm not a particularly weepy person, but I wept throughout this seven years like a broken water spout. We were either weeping or in paroxysms of giggles. We were obviously stretched absolutely taut.

When you came out did you think you'd been damaged?

Yes, I do think I was damaged. It took me about six years to recover from this, and I'm still not sure that I've altogether outgrown some of those things today, though I've learnt to compensate for them and use them in a different way. But for six years I existed in a state of grief. I was suicidal, I was anorexic, and just utterly, utterly depressed. I had no idea how to relate to people. It wasn't that I wanted to die so much as that I simply did not know how to live. The kind of training we had had in those day – it was a form of conditioning, a mild form of brainwashing. We'd be told to do something one day and the next we would be absolutely excoriated for doing it.

Was this to keep you obedient?

Obedient and not reliant on yourself, so that you would submit your will and judgement wholly to the will and judgement of your superior. It was very hard for me after I left the religious life to think at all. Even when I was a student at Oxford, I found it almost impossible to relate directly and spontaneously to a poem I was reading in English literature. Unless I found some critic – it didn't matter how miserable a critic or writer this might be – who said what I was struggling to articulate, I didn't feel I could have the idea.

You came out of the convent and you missed the 1960s. It wasn't just the rock 'n roll but a great many things of significance were happening in the '60s which were changing the social conscience and the way of life in our community. Did you find that very disorienting?

Yes, it was like having been Rip van Winkel, or someone who'd gone to sleep for a hundred years and come out and found an entirely changed society. We'd not been kept abreast of any of these developments. I'd never heard of the Beatles, for example, I'd never heard of Vietnam – and I left in 1969. So coming out and seeing youth protesting, demonstrating, when we'd not been able to voice a single objection in the convent. And the sexual revolution was underway – instead of the tight, polite little clothes we used to wear in the late 1950s, people had long scraggy hair and skirts right up to their thighs, this was just bewildering for me.

Did you declare yourself to be an atheist at this time?

I never went that far. To call yourself an atheist demands a degree of conviction and defiance and passion. I just fell away from religion, in an exhausted and wearied way. I felt sickened by it all. I had tried to open myself to God and God had wanted nothing to do with it. I realised I'd never believed much in this cosmic deity anyway and for about 13 years the whole idea of religion was utterly abhorrent.

And what was your moral principle then? What guided your behaviour, grounded you?

Most of these years were a struggle, a struggle to recover from the convent, also a struggle with undiagnosed epilepsy. I think kindness was one of the things that I began to value very, very much, the importance of treating other people kindly and with respect, which is not a great religious virtue I'm sorry to say. I began to feel that kindness was of crucial importance and in a sense it was that that eventually, by a long and circuitous route, brought me back to religion.

And then you wrote the book Through a Narrow Gate, *a very moving account of your life as a nun. Did that complete the story?*

Yes, it was redemptive I think. The first draft of that book was extremely angry so I had to dig down and remember things that had got buried under the anger and resentment. I began to realise how much of it I had valued. There had been one or two nuns in there, who'd been quite wonderful and who have remained luminaries for me. So it redeemed that time for me and laid it to rest, it was a closure.

Having written that book, you went to Jerusalem to make a television programme, and you began to see religion in a completely different light.

Yes. When you're living in Jerusalem, you cannot escape from other faiths. I had realised how parochial and limited my religious upbringing had been. I'd never thought of Judaism as anything but a kind of prelude to Christianity and I knew nothing about Islam at all, or Greek Orthodoxy. But surrounded by these different traditions, all jostling together in this small town, you become more aware of the hostility but also, the very real links that bind them together. In my subsequent work I have tried to develop what I once called triple vision, so that you see the three families as one tradition that went in three different ways, but none of them has the monopoly of truth.

Would you say that you discovered that your true calling is to be an academic devoted to scholarship and to write about what you discover?

Yes, I think my scholarship is a form of prayer. While I'm

studying and immersed in my books, I get moments of transcendence, or awe, or delight. Just mini-seconds. Now my
colleague, Lionel Blue, tells me that this is a very Jewish way
of praying, that this is what Jews do when they study Torah,
or Talmud. They don't speak to God in the way that Christians
often do but in the process of studying they will get glim-
mers of the divine. St Benedict had much the same idea. He
used to make his monks study, in the course of which they
would get mini-seconds of prayer. So I stumbled on this
form of spirituality.

What do you think religion is, what do you make of religion?

I see religion as an art form. Ever since we fell out of the
trees and became recognisably human, we created religion
and works of art to give us some sense that life has ultimate
meaning and value to make us wonder, to hold us in an
attitude of awe, because we're meaning-seeking creatures.
Without it we fall into despair very easily and art is one of the
things that transfigures reality for us, that makes us look more
clearly. I think you can see religion as a moral aesthetic. By
living in a certain way you transform yourself and I think
beliefs are neither here nor there.

*But if religion has been created by man to give meaning to the world,
is there any absolute meaning to the world and life, or is it just a
masquerade?*

There is meaning and it's not just a masquerade, any more
than art is masquerade but you can never articulate what that
meaning is, anymore than you can say exactly what a
Beethoven quartet means. You know that it affects you, you
know that it touches you deeply, lifts you beyond yourself
momentarily and gives you a sense that everything is at least

for this moment all right. If there's a world in which this can happen, it is all right. That is what the best of religion should be.

Is it built into our biological structure that we shall invent and believe in God?

Well, not all religions do believe much in gods. In the Buddhist tradition for example, gods are neither here nor there and in Hindu tradition, you could say the ritual is more important than the gods. But, you're right, our human mind is so constituted that we do have ideas and seek experiences that go beyond our grasp. We look for ecstasy, and if we don't find it in a church or synagogue or a mosque, we'll look for it in rock music, in theatre, music, drugs, sex, skiing even, sport, because we feel then, we are living most fully. Religion was for most people until the popularisation of art, one of the chief means whereby they got hold of this ecstasy that we need to make our lives meaningful.

So what do you make of the humanist/atheist tradition that has swept the West in which religion is seen to have been discredited? There are scientists who say it can't be proved and therefore where there is no evidence, there is no reality. Are we using the wrong vocabulary here?

Yes, we are. When you try and prove religious ideas and religious people themselves try and do this, it's a great mistake. You get bad religion and bad science. You can't prove the existence of God, and everybody always entirely understood this and nobody until the modern period when we started to think in wholly literalistic, scientific ways, ever thought that scripture was designed as literal truth. But I'd like to make a proviso; this distrust of religion is not the case in America.

America is the second most religious country in the world after India and it's not all fundamentalist by any means. The Americans – half of them at least – are engaged on a very exciting quest and a rebellion against some of the traditions that they feel are too limiting. They have a desire to think and worship in a more pluralistic way, and a hunger for religious affairs. When I talk in America, people will have tears in their eyes, whereas here, people will at best say, 'Well that's frightfully interesting', as though I were investigating the morals of an ancient Polynesian tribe. But in America, they don't think that religion is discredited. They're becoming more religious all the time.

You've written much about the three religions of the book: Christianity, Judaism and Islam. More recently you've written about fundamentalism in all of those religions and you say that all religions at some point in the twentieth century have had a fundamentalist strand.

It's just one of those developments. There are many types of religious expression but in the twentieth century, a militant form of piety grew up that was a rebellion against secular society. The first fundamentalist movement sprang up in the United States at the time of World War I. It didn't reach the Islamic world until a degree of modernisation had taken place in the late 1960s. Everywhere Western-style government has developed, a religious counter-culture has grown up alongside it wanting to drag God, the sacred, religion, back to centre stage. But also every single one of them has been a response to a perceived attack by secularists. Every single fundamentalist movement that I've studied in Judaism, Christianity and Islam is convinced that modern secular society wants to wipe them out. We must realise that fundamentalism has developed in a symbiotic relationship with a modernity and secularism that has been experienced as aggressive and invasive.

The vast majority of fundamentalists are simply trying to live what they regard as the religious life in a world that is increasingly hostile to religion and marginalises religion. The ultra-orthodox Jews in New York, for example, are not campaigning against the world, they're simply creating a sacred enclave where they can be Jewish as they see Judaism should be. A lot of the Islamic movements are like this too, a lot of the Christian fundamentalists in the United States are simply doing it. It's a fringe percentage – a tiny proportion – that take part in acts of terror and violence. First of all they are trying to reclaim their own patch for God. All fundamentalists – including Bin Laden – begin with an attack on their own society. Only in a secondary phase, if at all, do they take on a foreign foe.

Do you believe that the way you live moving easily between these different religions, is how we must live if we're going to understand each other?

Yes, we can no longer be religious as we were in the days when we didn't know about other traditions. One of the great gifts of the twentieth century was that for the first time in history, we had a real knowledge of other people's faith, not just their beliefs or their practices, but the faith that lay at the root of it. Now none of us can look at our own faith in the same way again. And I would agree with one of my great mentors, the Canadian scholar, Wilfred Cantwell Smith, himself a Christian minister, who said that it's now blasphemous to say that only one single tradition has the monopoly of truth, because we know so much more now.

Do you feel that with all these different concepts you explore in your religious writing, you have finally found a meaning?

I'm finding a meaning. Once you say, finally 'now I've got it', then you've lost it, because you're dragging it down to something very limited. It's an ongoing process and the meaning of it is the process itself. One is continually going into the depths of yourself, discovering a strength, a presence perhaps, in the heart of yourself.

And does it make you happy?

Yes it does. Somehow, after all the vicissitudes of my life, I've suddenly found the way in. I think we all have to follow our bliss as it were, follow the thing that fills you, not anybody else but you, with completion and delight.

❈

5

ANISH KAPOOR

'I feel very passionately that I do not have anything to say…'

Born in Bombay with a Jewish heritage from his mother, Anish Kapoor has lived and worked in Britain since the early 1970s. Over that period he has established and sustained a reputation as one of the most influential sculptors of his generation. He sees his work as engaged with metaphysical polarities: presence/absence, darkness/light. He won the Premio 2000 at the Venice Biennale in 1990. He won the Turner Prize in 1991. His recent piece Marsyas *for Tate Modern filled the turbine hall with its bold curving red shape. He seeks to evoke sublime experiences which address primal physical and psychological states. But in so doing, where does he place his own identity?*

Presumably at art school you are trained to put the brush on the canvas and the chisel into the stone … Does that still matter to you?

It matters to me a great deal. I love the sign of the hand. At the same time what one's saying is that the art that one's reaching to, the artifice that one's reaching through, doesn't necessarily have to be a record of my personality. One's talking about the notion that art might come to be beyond biography and come to be something that is reaching to a deeper part of our human presence.

Are you saying then that art is coming from somewhere else and that you are the vessel of the inspiration, or is it coming from your psyche?

Of course it's coming from one's psyche. There isn't anything else. But one's psyche may be the beginning of the story and not the end of the story. The idea is that somehow some fundamental transformation takes place in the process of doing this thing that we call making art, which leads to something else, something non-personal.

Something spiritual?

That's a word full of difficulties, but yes, something spiritual.

You see yourself as embarked on a lifetime as an artist, and there's a sort of coherence to your project that leads you decade upon decade to further a particular vision. Can you define it?

I think one defines it every day in the studio, one fumbles through it every day in the studio. But, given a small distance, I feel with some great certainty there is a big story in there somewhere. I've been working now I suppose for 20 years and I think I know some of that story. It opens up and I try to make my work continue to open it up. It is to do with this sense of the non-personal, the extra-personal. A kind of ... I hesitate to use the word 'alchemy'. Where one's working with physical objects, the alchemical in them isn't in their physics, it is the way that one is able or needs to project some kind of psychic matter into their manipulation that then leads to a third possibility that isn't either the matter or the psychic projection. Something else happens.

You hesitate to use the word 'God'. Perhaps it's a stumbling block. Is it appropriate?

It's too big and too complicated. Belief yes, faith yes, doubt yes. I think what I need to do as an artist, is to give all of those things space. I see myself as a non-narrative artist, I'm not trying to say anything. In fact, I feel very passionately that I do not have anything to say as an artist, that the moment that I do have something to say the game is lost, the space is closed up.

You become a propagandist?

Precisely. With all respect to journalists I do not wish to be a journalist. The role of an artist is to discover that which is outside of words or outside of the formed and of the thought.

You were born in India into the Hindu faith, your mother is of Jewish background; was this very evident in your childhood?

The most conspicuous thing about it for me is that I always felt like a foreigner. Although my father was a Hindu, he didn't believe at all, in fact he found Hinduism rather difficult. We had stronger connections to my mother's community and felt strongly part of it. Of course the two traditions that I grew up in are on the face of it complete opposites; one is a tradition without images, of the book so to speak, and of the family, and the other, Hinduism, is full of images, of the book too, but I think at its heart deeply abstract. I believe Hinduism to be about power, the power acquired from devotional activity of various kinds. That has been a great inspiration, an insight. I've learnt a great deal about the workings of the fundamental mystery of belief. As an artist I sense that one of the things that I'm working with is mystery, I sense also that we all have a deep need to believe. I think that process of wishing to believe is mysterious, it's one of the things I'm feeling my way towards.

When you were young, did you begin to share this mystery of the faith?

The short answer's 'no'. Neither of my parents are religiously motivated. Both my parents felt themselves to be atheistic in the everyday, but of a moral clarity that's wonderful. I felt as if I had to reclaim the territory of faith for myself alone and not being particularly courageous it has taken me a long time.

The liberal enlightenment seemed to believe that religion would fall away in the light of reason. But it hasn't happened and a spirituality of a new kind has emerged. How would you define that?

At one level it would appear that we are in crisis, that we think of ourselves, not just in Western society, but in all societies, as being in crisis. At another, we seem to be rediscovering a sense of a personal commitment to the spiritual, and that's for each individual alone. For me, when I came to this country in 1973, the shock of being here was enormous even though I'd grown up in a very cosmopolitan atmosphere.

A good shock or a bad shock?

Probably a bad shock. I suffered a difficult kind of breakdown which took me 12 years of analysis to overcome or to work through. That was a wonderful, incredible, marvellous awakening. A process I now with hindsight loved. What is interesting for me about psychoanalysis is that it is in a sense before religion. It is a process which helped me to reconstruct my image of myself. I had made the transition from an apparently blissful childhood, into this world that suddenly wasn't, and the process of reconstruction took a long time. But I knew that when the analysis, which was a deep and concentrated affair, was done with, I couldn't go any further. It's as if I'd constructed what I had to construct, and that the going beyond could only happen alone and outside of analysis.

And the journey still continues?

Absolutely.

And where is it taking you?

Well, for the last 10 years or so I have been an active Buddhist and felt that to be a very important part of my entity, mostly because it implies practice. Now, I believe in practice. Now going to the studio everyday is practice.

How do you practise your Buddhism?

In meditation, in increasing awareness of what one is. Self-consciousness perhaps. But while this is an important personal journey, Buddhism isn't something that defines what I do as an artist.

Does your Buddhism encompass a world view about what happens after death?

No.

You live without that?

It is one of those deep and fundamental mysteries that one has no answer to, that one can't find easy solutions to. What's important I think is to know where one's feet are right now, here and now. The rest will take care of itself.

Buddhism is one of the fastest-growing religions in this country. What is the quality of Buddhism that is so appealing?

At its heart it has that open space that we were talking about earlier on, and that contemplative space that insists on the now is one which by necessity has to be wide open. That appeals to us, it's not burdened with mythological baggage.

So let's talk about your art, because both the now and the place are dimensions of your work. So the Buddhist and the artist are in fact the same person?

Yes, they are. I do not want to make Buddhist art, because one can't. The only thing that I hold to is that the work comes out of continuous practice and application. Now much of my work is very sexual, yet at another level I have made much work that has no theme, that is in a sense space, void, empty. Both of those things run together and I don't see any conflict. I also don't see any need to push the work in one particular direction. It'll be what it is. Content, in other words, will and does arise of itself and I try and work with it.

One of the outstanding characteristics when your work first made an impact in the 1980s, was the colour that you used. Was that a deliberate use of your Indian background?

In some ways, although I don't want it to be exotic at all, I want it to be direct and not looked at for its foreignness. The wonderful thing about colour, is that it's completely non-verbal, that it has a direct route, it seems to me, to the symbolic, to the proto, the before words, the before thought, the thing in your gut, the visceral. That's something that is latently potent and we all possess it. I made a work about 10 years ago called *Descent into Limbo* (Mantegna). This consisted of a room, six metres cubed, built for the project; you walked into the room and there was a hole in the floor about a metre and a half in diameter. The hole was made in such a way that the perimeter fell away from the edge, so you had a sharp edge in the floor. The interior of this crevice was painted a very dark blue, blue that was perhaps read as being darker than any night, so in a sense the hole was filled with darkness. Now, people who went into this room were frightened standing on the edge of a precipice that feels as if it goes to the very centre of the earth. Why this work is important to me is that its darkness is witness to a darkness that we all know. It's darker than night. We carry it. We know it. It's as if what I was working with there was something which is common to us all, yet we can't name it and can't place it. I think one of the aspects of my so-called project is the notion of looking towards the interior, in a sense the eyes turned inwards. This implies all kinds of things about the meeting of interior and exterior, of the mysterious and the profane, of the mundane and the beyond.

You speak of art and your attitude to it in such a way as to suggest that art is a sort of new religion and that the artist is a priest for our time. Does that to make you feel self-conscious?

Yes, it does. However, there is something in it. One must never claim that role. That's why I try to argue for a non-auto-biographical art, one that comes to a condition of abstract certainty, that is available to the viewer at the same level to the initiated and the uninitiated. If it works for me it'll work for you.

Many of your objects are almost objects of contemplation in a reli-gious sense. Would you like your pieces placed in sacred spots?

Problematic. Art is very manipulative, specially sculpture. The process through which one directs the viewer to the expe-rience can be theatrical and can contextualise the course of how that experience is made. I would prefer the object to carry its own sense of place, its own sense of mystery, and somehow leave behind all of the trappings of church.

How important is it that art has a public life?

It has its role to play. It's important that visual culture in one way or another is more and more into our consciousness.

I just wonder if it isn't somewhere on the path to commodifying art, making it simply another of the commodities which we exchange.

The art market's never been so buoyant, there's never been in the art world such an obsession with youth and newness and all of that. Now these things, they're terrific, they lend energy to the situation. I think we must see them as a positive force. Money in these terms, for me anyway, tends to be irrelevant. If one of our young artists can sell work for a million or many millions, good luck, it's good.

I agree with that, but I really was seeking how the presence of your work is taking its place in a maelstrom of values in which money plays an increasing part. And this is a distortion of the distillation you're aiming for.

Money isn't a measure of value in art. Money is part of the mythology of art. The objects that artists make are signposts along the way to their mythological construction. That's what we're in the business of, making mythological constructions. Money's a wonderful part of that mythological construction, and is very effective. What you're suggesting is that money debases what is mysterious and potent in a work. I think not, I think it does the opposite. If one can see it as part of the mythological baggage, or package, it's a force that runs with the spiritual message of the work and not against it.

A word that hasn't been used so far is the word 'beauty'. Your work seems sublimely beautiful, almost effortlessly so – where does beauty figure?

Beauty is part of the engagement that one has as an artist. However, like the spiritual, it can't be sought for, beauty arises. I'm in my mid-forties. As I grow into what I've set for myself as an artist, I feel more and more comfortable with the notion of the beautiful. For a thing to be beautiful, first of all it needn't look beautiful. I think there's an implication of an inner life to the object. The other notion that occurs to me is one about recognition. For a thing to be beautiful we somehow need to play a game with the process of recognition, knowing and yet not knowing. Beauty isn't a static quality, it's something that occurs between the viewer and the viewed.

Do you see it around you, in the world in which you live?

The world is supremely beautiful, and the beautiful moments are almost always ephemeral. One can look at early Greek sculpture one day when the light is in a particular way and not find it beautiful, and go in another day when the light is in a different place and find it supremely beautiful; so it is between the viewer and the viewed.

What about the sublime, are you conscious of that in your life?

The sublime in art is all. It is mysterious and because it is not an aesthetic quality, it's not about how a thing looks, it's a condition that encompasses beauty but also encompasses fear. That's why I believe that looking at art is as difficult as making art and that one does need to educate oneself in order to look. It takes courage to make that leap, to allow that reverie, to suspend that disbelief, to fall in love.

❖

ROWAN WILLIAMS

'… the pebble dropped into the pool'

Rowan Williams is a poet, a scholar and the 104th Archbishop of Canterbury. He grew up in a Welsh-speaking home, and after degrees at both Oxford and Cambridge, he became a lecturer at The College of the Resurrection, Mirfield. He was ordained in 1978, took on academic and parochial work in Cambridge, then Oxford where in 1986 he became Lady Margaret Professor of Divinity. In 1992 he was made Bishop of Monmouth, and eight years later Archbishop of Wales. This interview was conducted in the December of 2001. In 2004 he was enthroned Archbishop of Canterbury. He has published two collections of poetry: Silent Centuries *and* Remembering Jerusalem.

Is poetry akin to the priesthood in extending your understanding of the universe and of yourself?

There's a sense in which I think poetry is an act of faith, an act of faith in language. You test the limits of language, you try to do and say new things, you make new connections in metaphors and you trust the language to carry on from there, to move on. And that's the excitement of it, not quite knowing what you find yourself saying but carrying on in the trust that it will enlarge, illuminate.

It's been said that in the secular world art fills a God-shaped hole.

To some extent it's true. I was in a discussion about Tate Modern as a modern cathedral, and I think that there is a sense that these are places for pilgrimage. They create moments where people have a sense that the world is larger and more confusing than they thought. Naturally I have some reservations about going along with that because I don't think secular art will quite do the trick. How does it open onto the future, or to use a word I don't much like, the transcendent?

Does poetry give you access to the spiritual whether you're a believer or not?

I think it gives a very profound access to the spiritual. And interestingly it does so by giving you another sort of access – to the physical – because poetry is about making noises, it's about doing things with your body, with your vocal chords, following rhythms and uncovering something in language itself.

When you're acting as a poet, do you feel different from when you're acting as a priest?

That's a difficult question to answer because I don't quite know what I'm doing when I'm acting as a poet. It sounds rather like walking down Piccadilly with a lily in my hand. But when I'm wrestling with the sheer difficulty, the intractability of how you pursue an image or a chain of words or a formal scheme of sounds, the kind of dead ends and brick walls you come up against, that you have to be prepared to look at and look through, then that's not a million miles from what you have to do when you're trying to pray.

You were born into a Welsh-speaking family, and brought up knowing both the religious tradition in Wales which is strong and rhetorical, and the Bardic tradition. Do they give you a particular take on your religious life?

There is something about growing up with a lot of Welsh around which makes you take language very seriously ... the sounds of the great preachers of the past, the sound of the great hymns. And such exposure as I had as a schoolboy to classical Welsh poetry, that certainly made a difference to a sense of how language worked and what it could be made to do. And because it's a very complex, rather sophisticated tradition, you see language being stretched to some very interesting limits in the iterative patterns of Welsh poetry and in the musical patterns of utterance in the Welsh pulpit.

You were an only child and suffered a good deal of ill health ... both isolating conditions.

Well, I learned to read quite quickly and that was it really. I read a lot and fairly indiscriminatingly. I remember finding mythology very interesting. It had something to do with the sense of landscape and environment as charged with strangeness. It was as if when you emerged from reading some kind of legendary stuff you would look around and think, well anything might happen in a landscape. And that moves into thinking about the world poetically as time goes on.

And do you use that eye from the pulpit?

When I'm preaching I think one of the most important things I can do is to try and touch the imagination. It's not an instruction, it's not just telling people to be nice, that would be awful. I hope that people will carry away from a good sermon a sense of the world being slightly larger.

Do you think everyone has such imaginative possibilities?

Yes, I do. There are all kinds of things in our educational system that do all they can to stifle that. It's one of the things that, sadly, institutional religion tends to do to people. It makes them very reluctant to share deep images. I find it very moving when people shyly and nervously begin to volunteer something of what really matters to them. When I was curate a man came to me trying to say what he felt as he was serving at the altar. Was it all right that he felt moved to tears when he was serving in the sanctuary? Was it all right? Of course it's all right! It's what it's about!

Early on in life you attended an Anglican church which had a very inspiring vicar.

Yes, his names was Eddie Hughes. He'd stayed in the parish about 26 years. When I was a teenager he got me to read Eliot and Auden, and for that matter Paul Tillich and theologians like that. I didn't ever feel when I brought up tiresome adolescent questions that I was being slapped down or patronised and that sense of being taken seriously matters a lot to spotty and tense adolescents. And his prayer life was so manifest. To be at a Eucharist he celebrated you knew that there was something very serious going on.

Did you play your part in the congregation?

I was a very keen singer, so I was in the choir. I did find that church was one of the things that made the world look larger and brighter.

You didn't have adolescent doubts then?

I didn't, no. Partly because at every stage where things seemed to be getting more complicated, I felt there was an environment to grow into, there was room to move within the scheme, within the system of worship and talk.

So your intellectual life has been within the parameters of belief throughout?

Yes, it has. There've certainly been times when it's felt as if the boundaries have been pushed quite hard. But that adolescent feeling that this is a very large room and that it can keep pace with whatever intellectual growth and questioning is taking place in me, that stuck with me and perhaps affected some of the ways I think about theology in general.

You studied at both Cambridge and Oxford before you became a priest and a teacher, a don. How about encounters with science, with the Darwinian revolution, with the scholarship of the historic story of Jesus?

When I first came across the historical critical approach to the Bible my instincts were to be rather suspicious and it took a while to work through that. When I began to realise that this was a way of giving you reading skills, not just a hostile undermining, then it was a bit of a breakthrough. When I was studying theology at Cambridge the people who mattered to me were the people who were able to make of the historical critical method something that took you further into the heart and life of the text rather than pushing it further away. I think that can be done.

The Darwinian thing is a bit more difficult. But I think quite early on, what I read and studied about the nineteenth century made me feel that whatever the Darwinian revolution was, it wasn't intrinsically a revolution in how you ought to think about ethics and theology. Rather it posed huge questions as to what you might want to say about the essentially human.

Scholarship tells us that the Bible was written by many hands at different periods and the texts selected by churchmen several hundred years after Christ. What does that do to a simple faith that the Bible is the word of God?

I think it's quite important that at no point in Christian history have Christians decided that the Bible is like the Koran, a direct dictation from God. There has always been a sense that there are levels in it. There are even conflicts. But there's an agenda. Bishop Westcott in the nineteenth century said the Bible was there to remind us what spiritual life was about. You had to work at making sense of it.

Well, you have laboured at it. What do you believe it to be?

I believe the Bible to be the primary record of the impact of God's action on a set of human communities and the primary record of where the impact comes to its climax in the life and death and resurrection of Jesus Christ. So it's much more a set of people reacting with excitement, bewilderment, puzzlement, imagination to what's been going on, rather than a simple linear communication from God. God acts, the world changes, people struggle to find the words that express that change. And the important thing about the New Testament is that it's work in progress, it's the debris of an explosion, it's people confusedly trying to make sense of something that has altered the parameters very very dramatically.

We don't update the New Testament, do we? We might change its language but we don't update the theology?

We don't update the theology precisely because of that character of primary disturbance. This is where the pebble dropped into the pool, this is where the turbulence starts from.

Does what you say extend to the Old Testament? How do you deal with the cruelties of God there: Abraham being required to sacrifice his son, for example? The Israelites being urged to slaughter their enemies?

The way I've thought about this is that the impact of God on people is not always kindly. It is not always the opening of a flower. It can feel like a blow. It can feel like an explosion of the mind. It can lead people to do terrible things as well as astonishing, courageous and compassionate things. And it's only as the story builds up, as the sense of the character of God gradually comes into focus that the impact stops being quite so potentially horrific. It's quite important to recognise that in the early stages of biblical narrative the sense of what's called the divine wrath, the divine jealousy, the impact of the sheer difference and oddity of God can distort and warp people.

Many people reject this jealous wrathful God and simply say 'How can I worship such a God?' What has held you rooted to your belief?

Two things: one is watching what happens in the whole evolution and development of the Bible's language. The second is listening to people who have done the reading throughout the centuries and you see what happens to them. I think historically what Christians have done is say 'Well, read the Bible as a whole and it's quite clear that God is not, in the whole pattern of divine action, hostile to particular groups of people.' Nor does he, at the end of the day, authorise violence and exclusivism towards other ethnic groups. If we mean what we say about God, that God is that on which the world depends, then one thing you can't say about God is that God is one agent among several. And that means that God isn't ever competing for space with bits of the world and that God is therefore not in that sense a jealous God or in rivalry with the bits of the world. The action of God is consistent and steady all the way through.

When it comes to the New Testament, Christians have been in disagreement with two matters: the Virgin Birth and the bodily Resurrection. Are they metaphorical stories?

No, I don't think they are. At the beginning of the story of the virginal conception of Jesus, there is the bare fact being asserted that Jesus had no human father. At the end of the story there's another bare fact being asserted, that there wasn't a body in the tomb or anywhere else. Now these two huge absences, the beginning and end of Jesus' story, seem to me to be vastly significant absences, the sort of absence, darkness, mystery where God is found.

What I'm not going to the stake for is whether every detail of 1st chapter, Matthew and 20th chapter, John is precise reporting. I go back again to this sense that what people are doing in the New Testament is floundering round trying to find the words, so that over a generation a pattern of stories builds up, based on a set of perfectly real experiences and a perfectly real state of affairs. But what we haven't got is a tidy report filed at the end of Easter Sunday.

So any attempt to verify the historical truth about Jesus is a cul-de-sac?

I think there is interesting and constructive work you can do on what Jesus is likely to have meant by this, that or the other. There are outlines of Jesus' earthly activity that you can uncover. But I don't think you'll ever get a perspective-free story. And I don't know if that gets you very much further forward.

If I were to bring in the word 'myth' here – knowing that this is a hugely misleading word – there's a sense in which what Christians hold to as they worship isn't a set of distant facts about Jesus, but the way those facts have been picked up, seen through, patterned. So what you have is a version of what the universe is like with the face of Christ as its centre. And, thinking about it, I'd rather use the word 'icon' than 'myth'.

There is seen to be a paradox in your beliefs, because while holding traditional views of dogma, you are perceived as holding liberal views about such matters as women priests, gay priests, even women bishops.

I think it's a great pity the Church has come to be identified in most people's minds with a set of knee-jerk reactions around various issues of sexuality. I don't think it helps much if the Church pins its identity on that issue. Issues about women, about the role of gay people in the Church, seem to me to be issues of how seriously you take the inclusiveness of God's core and a willingness to let at least some elements of experience affect the ideology. So if you see a woman who is praying quite deeply within fairly traditional forms who is apparently growing as a human being before God and discerns a call to ministry, I don't want to write that off. That's the kind of consideration I want to have about gay people, that if you have someone who is seriously praying, seriously thinking, whose life shows some evidence of the fruits of the spirit, I don't think it answers anything just to say we can't think about that. It's really a matter of looking, or trying to look at the wholeness of life here. Is this a life that's lived responsibly? A life that tries to respond to mystery?

But these differences are now pushing at the frontiers: gays now speak of gay marriage, women want to be bishops. Do you feel you have to draw the line somewhere?

I find it difficult to draw the line in advance. I want to think of these things as they arise and try to bring some theological resource to them and get the Church out of the habit of being anxious about this all the time.

If you were asked to conduct a gay marriage what attitude would you take?

I'd have to say no. I'm somebody under authority. I have made public vows about observing what can and can't be done in public worship. What I might say is, if you want me to pray for you, I'll do that. But I can't do more.

You bring scholarship and thought to your faith. What do you think of the Charismatic approach which sees prophesying and speaking with tongues as a kind of faith that doesn't call on any intellectual thoughts?

I've actually learned a lot from the Charismatic movements and would say I'm personally grateful to them for enlarging my understanding and deepening my prayers.

And speaking in tongues?

I think it's one of those things that happens under certain kinds of spiritual pressure. You'll find records of it in early Christian writers and in the Middle Ages. It's not just a modern phenomenon. But if the impact of God does knock you sideways in some ways there can be some very odd physiological results as well as mental results.

Do you believe in miracles?

I see no reason why the action of God shouldn't at some point break through where the fabric of the world thins out a bit and the action of God is nearer the surface. Exactly how that happens is inscrutable to us. We can't make a science out of it. But I think I'd be confident enough to say I've seen sufficient to believe that the action does come through in certain instances.

And prayers are answered?

Prayers are answered. Or prayer in some way helps to thin out the fabric of the world or opens the door of opportunity for the action of God to come through.

People might ask why a miracle for some person and not another, one person's prayers answered and not another?

As a believer, I know there are two or three things I'm pretty certain of: that we are instructed to pray for people and outcomes; that it is in principle possible for the action of God to come through; and that there can be some connection between the two but we're not going to know what it is. If we simply see God as deciding here and there to intervene and saying 'I can't be bothered with that one', that's awful, and makes for an arbitrary God. What I'm trying to think through in respect of prayer is that somehow in the world as it is, God acts when the conditions are there. What makes the conditions there, isn't a map I can fill out in every respect.

We live in a world of many faiths. Is it difficult for someone as grounded in your Christian faith and the Anglican Communion as yourself to acknowledge the equality of other faiths and traditions?

I think equality could mean two things. It could mean equality in civic terms and in terms of sheer ordinary human respect. And I don't have any problem about that. It can mean equality in the sense of 'well this is what I see and that's what you see, and who knows?' And that disables real conversation.

The one true faith in the sense that there is one social order, one institution in which all truth is held, I think is impossible to sustain. That the world is as Christian doctrine depicts it, I believe. How people of other faiths, traditions find room in that is very challenging and a rather exciting thing to work at with people of other traditions. They would say, of course, exactly the same about me.

7

PAUL DAVIES

'... the universe is about something ...
it is not just arbitrary and absurd.'

Paul Davies is a scientist with an enormous sweep of interests. His research extends across the fields of cosmology, gravitation and quantum field theory, with particular emphasis on black holes and the origin of the universe. He is also interested in the nature of time, high-energy particle physics, and the nature of consciousness. He has held academic appointments in astronomy, physics and mathematics in the universities of Cambridge, London, Newcastle upon Tyne and Adelaide and is currently Professor of Natural Philosophy in the Australian Centre of Astrobiology at Macquarie University, in Sydney.

He is also a prolific writer about science having published over 25 books, both popular and specialist, most famously, The Mind of God, About Time *and* The Origin of Life. *He was made a Fellow of The Royal Society of Literature in 1999. In 2002 he was awarded the Michael Faraday Prize by the Royal Society for his promotion of physics to the public. His title,* The Mind of God, *is taken from the final sentence of Stephen Hawking's book* The Meaning of Time, *and I ask whether we can read into it an indication of his own belief.*

❖

It's an indication of the belief of many scientists, particularly physicists, that there is a real order in the world out there and that in doing our science we are uncovering the way the world really is. The early scientists like Galileo and Newton supposed that what they were doing was uncovering God's handiwork for the world. Although in the minds of most scientists we've killed God off, I think the notion of something 'out there', something ordered and rational and intelligible that we uncover through doing science, remains prevalent among scientists including those who would call themselves atheists.

Have you now arrived at your beliefs or are you always in a state of re-believing the more you discover?

As a scientist I'm always prepared to change my mind when there is new evidence or new ideas. But I think it's really important that we adopt a spirit of openness and the possibility of progress in the realm of the spiritual just as we do in science and technology. After all the last 300 years have witnessed an enormous advance in science, technology, material well-being, health and economics. But most people's ideas of religion or spirituality tends to be rooted in the past. In some cases in ancient texts that were written 2000 years ago. They don't seem to have moved on very much.

You sound as though you're constantly revising what you think.

Well, I take these things seriously and you're quite right. Most people are exposed to religious ideas at a rather naïve level in their childhood and then when they get to their late teens and have to think about building a career, getting married, bringing up families and so on, they really don't have time to think through the issues involved in the deep questions of existence. And for those few people who still go to church or some other religious institution, that's the job of the priest. They're there to give you the answers. I'm fortunate that I've been able to make a career as a scientist and as a philosopher and I have had time to reflect on these fundamental issues. I spend a lot of time travelling around the world talking to other people who are doing the same, and I'm completely open-minded.

Let's go back then to your own childhood and how the ideas that you hold now have arisen from then.

My parents were religious in a fairly conventional way which meant the Church of England. I joined the Cubs and went to Sunday school and church parade. I always felt virtuous when I went to church but terribly bored. By my teens, of course, like all teenagers I was rebelling and questioning all these things. I did join a church youth club, largely to meet the girls and from time to time the curate from the church would come along to the youth club and we'd have a discussion about something deep and meaningful. By about the age of 16 when I had entered the Sixth Form at school and I was studying physics and mathematics, I began seriously to question what all this church business was about.

The fact that you took for granted that the world was explained by the Christian ideology and the Christian story, must have influenced your values from very early on.

It did. Let me say one thing and I think it's really important. Whatever we may conclude about church attendance and theological issues and science and religion, there is one way in which living as we do in a notionally Christian community has affected me and everybody else and that concerns Christian values. Quite independently of what I thought about the Bible or theological issues, I grew up with a very clear idea of the difference between right and wrong and the importance of Christian ideals like loving your enemy even if it meant something trivial like clapping the other side when they scored a goal. Those things never leave you and even in a country like Britain, where most people have abandoned going to church, nevertheless I think they still subscribe to broadly speaking Christian ethics. Christianity doesn't have a monopoly on virtuous behaviour but certainly having a framework of moral and ethical ideals was important to me, and has been important in shaping who I am.

In these turbulent adolescent years were you confronted by serious and alarming doubts or by the thrill of discovery?

The formative time was probably when I was about 16 – maybe 17 – in the Sixth Form, beginning to learn some more advanced physics and mathematics and worrying about things like free will and determinism. I think I saw that if I really was interested in issues like the mind-body problem, I'd have to become a physicist. I was particularly influenced by reading two books more or less simultaneously. The first was by Fred Hoyle, the British cosmologist, called *Frontiers of Astronomy*, a wonderfully refreshing and exciting look at the then emerging subject of cosmology. And at the same time I read John Robinson's *Honest to God*, which was a similar attempt to rebuild theology. Robinson sought to demolish the notion of God as a cosmic magician or an old man in the sky. And I thought well it is possible to look at these really deep issues of existence of science and of theology in a spirit of open-minded enquiry and research. I thought this was wonderfully thrilling. I saw it as a great open opportunity to question all of the things that people thought must be already decided.

Did you feel that the world that you were abandoning, the supernatural elements of the Christian faith which you'd taken for granted, left you with a sense of loss?

Yes, there has been a sense of loss, but compensated to some extent by the wonder that science has presented to me. The fact that science exposes a universe of such thrilling and stunning ingenuity and beauty is so inspirational. This is really a glimpse of what we might call 'God the grand architect', the grand designer – a remote abstract entity, not the personal God of popular religion, not the God who's going to respond to prayer.

Did you suffer doubt and depression at there not being truth to the Christian explanation?

I've always been an optimist. With science itself you have to be optimistic because you've got to believe that we're going to discover new things, make progress and that the fruits of science are not going to destroy us all. And like everybody else I have periods of depression as I get older because of course I think about my own mortality. Some small part of me thinks, 'well existence is so extraordinary that maybe continued existence after death would be no more extraordinary.' But as a scientist, it's very hard for me to regard immortality as a realistic prospect. I think conventional religion is a comfort to people. I think it fulfils a social and psychological function and I don't want to belittle that. But by the age of 16 or 17 I'd gone beyond feeling that it was something that I needed as a psychological prop. I really wanted to see if there was anything deeper. I take theology and spirituality very seriously but I don't go to church, I don't attend acts of worship. The trappings of religion are so incredibly powerful: the hierarchy, the buildings, the combination of architecture, science, music and religion all coming together. I think the trappings of religion are tremendously inspiring. That's why they're so powerful.

You use and explore the vocabulary of religion itself in your scientific explanation. For example, you are very up-front about the use of the word God. What do you mean by God?

I'm not alone in doing this. You go to a physics conference and people will sit around and they'll often talk about God or maybe Nature with a capital N, or Mother Nature even. To be a scientist you really do have to believe that there is a world out there that is ordered in a rational and intelligible way and that what we are involved in is a voyage of discovery, that we're trying to figure out actual properties of nature. I believe we're reading these properties *out of* nature not imposing them *on* nature. Some people contend that science is just an exercise in inventing human categories and projecting them onto nature. I think that is wrong. I believe there is a really-existing order in nature that we discover through doing science. There's something clever, something really ingenious, rational and intelligible out there in nature and the word 'god' seems to encapsulate that very well.

Whereas in fact what you are saying is that science is God?

Well, I wouldn't want to say that science is in some sense a religion or a substitute for religion. I don't think people should look to scientists in the same way as they look to priests. But when it comes to the physical universe I think that unquestionably science is the way to go. And I include in that the origin of the universe, the Big Bang that started it all off. A lot of people want to find God in the Big Bang or before the Big Bang. I think that's a deep mistake. That's not the place to look for God. The one thing you must beware of is the so-called 'god of the gaps', the idea that because scientists at this particular time can't explain this or that phenomenon then we must wheel in a god to plug the gap. That's been the way it's worked for hundreds of years and of course God has got successively squeezed out of the gaps until he's more or less pushed right back to the beginning of the universe to the Big Bang itself and that's the only place that you need this poor old God.

You say 'it's not the right place to look for God,' suggesting that the search for God is a legitimate intellectual activity.

Oh yes, I don't think there is any doubt about that but the god we are talking about is not a cosmic magician, not some miracle working super being up there in the sky and especially not a god-of-the-gaps.

So what is God?

The first thing you conclude if you're a physicist or cosmologist is that time is part of the physical universe. Einstein showed us that. Time is not a backdrop. Space and time together don't form, as Newton thought, an arena in which the universe happens, in which the great drama of nature is acted out. They're part of the cast, space and time can change and move.

Is there something before time?

People always want to ask that and of course by definition there is nothing before time. Stephen Hawking has expressed this rather well by comparing it with the question of what lies north of the North Pole. Well you can answer 'nothing lies north of the North Pole'. That's not because some mysterious Land of Nothingness lies there, it's because there's no such place as 'north of the North Pole'. In the same vein there's no such time as 'before the Big Bang' because the Big Bang was the origin of time, at least in a simple picture of cosmology (and I have to caution that many cosmologists now do not think the Big Bang was necessarily the absolute origin of the entire physical universe). Now people think that answer is just a trick – a way of getting God out of the picture by saying that it's meaningless to talk about the prior epoch. But already in the fifth century St Augustine said that the world was made 'with time and not in time'. I think this is an absolutely crucial point.

What it means is that if we want to talk about God we've got to talk about a being, an entity that is *outside of time* and if what we are after is an explanation for the universe, then that universe *includes* time and space. So the explanation for the universe must lie within something that *transcends* time and space. While that makes a physicist feel very comfortable, it's not much comfort for those people who want a god who can dip into the running of the universe from time to time. The timeless God I am describing must be contrasted with the old-fashioned God – a superbeing who sits there for all eternity and who, at some particular moment decides, 'I'll have a universe!' and then presses a button and – bang! – the universe appears. And then maybe from time to time this superbeing prods the universe by moving atoms around. I find this old-fashioned, but still popular concept of God offensive both scientifically and theologically.

And a God that sends his son to redeem people?

That is of course absolutely crucial for Christians. That is the one point where you cannot duck the issue about God intervening in nature. There are various episodes in the development of the universe that a lot of people feel that require God as the explanation. I find it repugnant on both theological and scientific grounds to have a god who meddles on an occasional basis acting like a force of nature in competition with the other forces of nature. That's not where to look for God at all. 'No miracles other than the miracle of Nature itself!' is my mantra. I think it's quite wrong to vest too much significance in the origin of things and in particular the Big Bang. It's more fruitful to look at the underlying laws, the laws of physics which explain all this. We can now understand how the laws of physics can bring the universe into existence from nothing, can bring space and time into existence where there was no space or time, where there was literally nothing. We can understand that that is not necessarily a supernatural act, it could be a natural process. This is very significant because people used to suppose that the originating event itself cannot be brought within the scope of science. However I think we *can* have a thoroughly scientific account of the universe at all times including the ultimate origin of things. But you still have a right to ask, 'Where did these laws come from? Why those laws and not some other set? Is there anything special or peculiar about the actual laws?'

And also is there a purpose behind this creation?

If you ask me what do I mean by this word 'God', I would say something like 'the rational ground in which is rooted the wonderful laws that can bring a universe into existence and bring life and reflecting beings like ourselves into existence.' It strikes me that there is something purpose-like, design-like, goal-like in all of this. These words are of course loaded because they are taken from human discourse and projected onto nature. We have to be very careful how we use them. But nevertheless I think it's legitimate to say that in some sense the universe is *about* something, it's not just arbitrary and absurd. It would be wrong to suppose that human beings are the pinnacle of creation or at the centre of the universe. But we're not insignificant either.

We're not just specks whirling in space?

No. The existence of mind, the fact that we can come to understand the world through science and intellectual enquiry is of tremendous significance. The more I look at it the more convinced I am that our own intellectual capabilities link in to the deepest processes of the universe in a way which is not accidental. So if we want to be very crude about it and say there is a plan or purpose to the universe, then I think we are part of that plan, a modest part not a central part, but never the less a significant part.

You have written that people hold beliefs, especially in the field of religion, which might be regarded as irrational but that they are held irrationally doesn't mean that they are wrong.

Most physicists rather arrogantly assume that their techniques are going to reveal everything, that all of existence can in principle be explained this way. But I'm actually rather sceptical that that is the case. There may be areas of human enquiry that simply won't yield to those sorts of methods. At the end of the day what really matter are things like our personal freedom, our feelings for other people, love and so on, our fear of death and what lies beyond. And frankly science has done rather little to touch upon those things except to either sweep them under the carpet or try to define them away.

How much is your behaviour governed by the set of beliefs you hold?

Where I increasingly find myself – or at least my judgements – being coloured by science is less from physics, more from biology. Recognising that I am an animal, that I have evolved, that my mind, my wishes and desires have been shaped by evolution and that there might be sound evolutionary reasons sometimes for something of a rather prosaic nature that determines the way I feel about things. The rather contentious subject of evolutionary psychology, which is still in its formative stages, is actually very useful for helping us to understand human nature and to assist in making judgements particularly about things like criminal behaviour before we rush to condemn. It really is useful to see the biological basis for some of this.

And free will?

Oh that's what got me started on this great quest! Have we really got freedom? You wear one hat – the physicist hat – and it looks as though free will is either non existent or meaningless. And then you go off to do day-to-day chores and of course you act as if you have freedom....

You say 'as if'....

It is 'as if'. It's very hard to pin down whether free will is a meaningful thing. Is it just a feeling we have, or can we actually change the world? Is there a genuine openness in the evolution of the world through which sentient beings can act.

I'm still undecided on this issue, I keep going around and around in circles. It's part and parcel of the great mystery of consciousness. The actual sensations we get of the world – the things that philosophers call *qualia*, the redness of red and the greenness of green and so on – are still deeply mysterious. I see free will as part of that mystery. I really haven't made up my mind on that one yet. I'm still working on it.

8

FATHER TIMOTHY RADCLIFFE

'… the pilgrimage to truth'

Father Timothy Radcliffe OP was for nine years – from 1992 to 2001 – Master General of the Dominican Order of the Catholic Church worldwide. He was born into one of England's recusant Catholic families that held to their faith throughout the major Protestant persecutions of earlier centuries. He went to Downside School, where he was taught by Benedictines, but chose to be a Dominican, entering the Order at the age of 20. He was a chaplain, theologian and teacher before, in 1988, he was elected English Provincial. He is an international preacher and speaker, based at Blackfriars, Oxford.

I think it's important that faith starts with reason, and that's not reason in some narrow sense of just doing logic. It's all the ways that human beings try to make sense of their experience, and that's through philosophy, but it's also through art and poetry and plays and so on. Faith embraces all the sense that we have of the meaning of our lives but leads us beyond that to the ultimate meaning which is God.

But does the world of reason posit a different set of thinking that runs adjacent to faith, that might be in tension with it?

I wouldn't say so, no. I think faith embraces all of our

humanity and that includes our power to struggle to understand. So if I read the Bible as a Christian in faith, in the light
of faith, that doesn't mean to say I'm going to put aside any of
the powers of reason or logic that I have.

*But reason might say that many of the things in the Bible are not
reasonable. It doesn't bear proof.*

I would say that it might take us beyond reason but it would
never be against reason. Faith is not irrational. God made us to
know him and we know him through the transformation of
our reason and not by its abolition.

*Many Catholic families are descended from those recusant Catholics
who suffered for their faith in times of persecution. So there's a
subversive element in the Catholic Church isn't there?*

Absolutely. I think it's essential to the identity of Catholicism that our ultimate loyalty is not to the state. And that's
why when I became involved in the peace movement some of
my family were rather scandalised because we were sometimes committing acts of civil disobedience. But to me this was
in continuity with what my ancestors had got up to. We have
an allegiance to humanity rather than just to the state of Great
Britain. It doesn't mean that we are against the community in
which we live, it's just not our ultimate community. Our ultimate community is humanity which is ultimately the
Kingdom of God.

Does that put it at odds with the sovereign state?

Yes, it would if you found that the community in which we
happened to live acted in a way that was discriminating
against other human beings, if we came across racism for

example, then our fidelity to the Kingdom would obviously override our allegiance to that particular community.

You grew up in a family steeped in the Catholic faith: what did that feel like?

It felt very natural. We were deeply religious in the sense that it was assumed that God is good, God wills our happiness and with his grace we're on the way to heaven. But we weren't at all devout or pious. Like most children we hated going to mass, we had the giggles and went to sleep during the sermon. It wasn't a strict and rigid religion. I would say we had a sense that faith was joyful.

What was your daily life like? Was mass said every day?

Only when we had priests staying. We often had priests staying in the house and then we'd be drummed up to serve their mass. We had quite a lot of relatives who were Benedictines. I had a great uncle who was a Benedictine, who'd come and stay with us. He was exuberant, filled with life. He used to love his wine and late in the evening he would demand his whisky. One never thought of priests as being austere people who hated life.

And when you went to boarding school at Downside?

I would say all the monks came across as human, except for when we were beaten, which seemed to be quite often. For smoking, escaping to the pub, that sort of thing. I was caught reading *Lady Chatterley* when it was a banned book. During benediction, I'm ashamed to say.

How did you come to make the choice of being a friar?

When I left school, before university, for the first time I

made non-Catholic friends, in fact friends who weren't Christians at all, and they challenged my belief. They said that Catholicism was a superstitious religion and that I should free myself from it. For the first time I had to ask the question 'Is it true?' And it became an almost obsessive question. Either it's true, in which case it's the most important thing that could be. Or it's not true, in which case I should leave the Church. I remembered that a religious order had the motto 'truth'. So I telephoned the Benedictines and asked the Abbott, an old friend of mine, 'Which is the order committed to truth?' He said the Dominicans. So I made an appointment to see the Provincial. I had decided to be a Dominican before I ever met one.

So what was the answer to your friends who challenged you as to whether your faith was true or not?

I have come now to understand that it is indeed true, but the truth is never something we master and dominate. The more I enter into understanding the truth, the more I've also learned a certain humility in the face of other faiths.

Does truth mean that events happened literally as they are related in the Bible?

It sounds as if you are appealing to a rather late nineteenth century understanding of literalism, which of course the writers of the Gospels never had. I think the modern idea of literalism really only came in the light of a certain development in science, when you lost all other senses of the ways in which texts have meaning – metaphorically, analogically. I think the Gospel writers had a much richer sense of truth than we tend to.

*Some people have sought to verify the Bible by searching the archae-
ology for evidence. They've gone looking for Noah's Ark, they've
looked for Golgotha, they examine the Temple Mount.*

That's good because they're trying to help us understand in
what sense the text is true. For example if you look at the
Resurrection, which I obviously believe to be true – the bodily
resurrection from the tomb – if it turned out that they found
the body of Jesus, then my faith in the Resurrection would be
undermined. But I wouldn't find that, if we didn't find Noah's
Ark. That wouldn't undermine my faith. The resurrection of
Christ isn't the disappearance of the body, it's the victory of
life over death. It's the victory of love over hatred. The disappearance of the body is the sign, an absence that points to
something infinitely deeper and more important.

So we're not talking symbolic stories here?

Well some stories are symbolic and some aren't.

Who's to decide?

The Church, the community, by reflecting together.

But some might think one thing, some another.

That's the wonderful thing within the Church. It's by disagreement that we eventually arrive at some common
understanding.

*But doesn't disagreement lead to heresy? The Dominicans, after all,
played a part in the Inquisition.*

Not necessarily. I think without disagreement you never
deepen your faith. There were many inquisitions and the Dominican order wasn't the only order involved. I think at that
stage maybe we were operating with too narrow an idea of

veritas, truth. The temptation is to think that you've mastered it, you know it all. But it doesn't mean we don't believe in debate and disagreement. I think it's at the heart of our faith.

Is there only one truth above all others?

Well, finally, there is one truth in which we all meet. I sometimes think when I'm talking with somebody, I might want to say 'You're wrong.' But that doesn't mean you're totally wrong and it's almost never the case that I'm totally right. The challenge is to discover the sense in which the other person is right. St Thomas Aquinas – perhaps the greatest theologian in the Christian tradition – always starts every discussion by looking at the objections. He always asks, 'Is there any sense in which they are true?' Because we're on the pilgrimage to truth until we arrive at the Kingdom.

Do you feel, then that all religions are true but mine is truer than others?

I believe in the truth of my faith but I do not believe I own the truth of God. The truth of God is beyond anything I can ever say or know.

Is your God the Muslim God, the Hindu God, the Sikh God?

The truth of God is beyond all the Gods that we think we know. St Thomas Aquinas said 'What God is, we cannot know.' This means that when I meet a Muslim or a Hindu, I go to share what I believe, but I also go as a beggar. I go to learn and I go with open hands. Because if I'm attentive enough the Muslim, the Buddhist, the Hindu will teach me about God, will teach me about Christ.

You took vows of poverty, chastity and obedience, and you've spoken about the sense of freedom that gave you. How freeing is it to take a vow of obedience?

It depends what you think freedom is about. If it's about choosing between alternatives, that's a very superficial freedom. As a Dominican I will never own a Rolls-Royce for example. And I'm told where to live. But I discovered the freedom of giving my life to the brethren. And it's never blind obedience: it's always mutual. Superiors have to listen to what the brethren say and we always try to reach a consensus.

The vow of chastity means a loss of that intimate one-to-one relationship that makes many peoples' lives worth living. Did you have to mourn that loss?

Well, in some sense you don't lose it. You can't ever have that privileged relationship of being the most important for one person in the world. You never have what I imagine is a beautiful experience of going to sleep with somebody and waking up with them. And I think that is a real loss. But you don't renounce loving other people. You don't renounce intimacy. Chastity should free you to love the people who don't get loved much. I'm often moved by our sisters in the slums of Latin America, in AIDS clinics in Africa. They love the people who don't receive too much love.

We live in times when men and women are gaining the right to be treated as equals. But the Catholic Church will not ordain women. Why?

First of all you have to look at what it means to be a priest. The traditional argument is that if somebody is to represent the person of Christ they should be a man as he was. Personally I don't think that this is an absolutely convincing argument. I think you have to look at much deeper questions about what it means to be male and female. What is the significance of gender? And we're just at the very beginning of exploring that as a society, let alone as a church.

We're divided into male and female, thanks be to God. But we have also to discover complementarity. What is it that men can receive from women? And we're at the beginning of the adventure of discovering that.

We're at the beginning of many things, including the march of science towards an understanding of more and more of the cosmos, and the nature of consciousness. What do you say to the scientist who maintains there is no 'meaning of life', we just are?

Well, a scientist's free to say that but when he does he's moved beyond his remit as a scientist. He's moving into the area of faith and he can make such a statement as a person who believes or doesn't believe. If as a theologian, I say 'the world was created in six days, literally', I move beyond the area of my responsibility into what's the responsibility of the scientist. Now you have scientists who believe, and theologians who are scientists, so we often have dual identities. But we have to respect the difference between the disciplines and I believe there is no inherent contradiction. There's no sense in which theology limits the exploration of science.

Where there might be tension is in examining the idea of life after death.

When Christians talk about life after death, we're not just talking about some ethereal existence like ghosts. We're talking about entering into the fullness of life and that is something we don't just do when we die. We start doing that now. If you love someone deeply you start to enter into the fullness of life now.

When someone you love dies, you have a sense that that fullness has been destroyed.

Certainly. It's been deeply wounded. So I don't think that questions about life after death are resolved by looking for ghosts. To understand Christian teaching about life after death you have to begin by understanding what it means to be fully alive now.

Have you been present at many deathbeds?

Yes, I think it's one of the final gifts people can give us, their way of dying. Some of my brethren have died beautifully, with joy, with laughter, they've faced this moment transparently and with courage. That's a wonderful gift to give people, isn't it?

Do you think the heart of the Christian message is that Christ came and destroyed death?

I think he destroyed all that suffocates humanity. At the Last Supper when he gave his body and blood to the disciples he embraced suffering, death, their betrayal, hatred: all that diminishes our humanity. And he overcame that. And that means the infinity of desire that inhabits every human being – and every human being really longs for infinity – that desire will not be frustrated.

You speak with conviction but tell me about your doubts.

I don't think I ever doubted the existence of God. But I've had moments where God seemed very distant. I went through a period when I was a young Dominican which was really very sterile. Intellectually I had given assent to the existence of God. Though I had got bored. But I just had to hang in there. If you have periods of aridity you just have to hang in there. You have to keep moments of silence where you wait to hear God's voice.

What pulled you through?

I think a passion for study. I never lost that. Reading everything I could lay my hands on: poetry, philosophy, sociology, everything. I think it was my passion to understand. I kept that. And the other thing was the friendship of my brethren, the love of my brethren.

And moments of truth?

Oh, moments of illumination. One day shortly after I was ordained a priest I was in Jerusalem, in the Garden of Gethsemene when suddenly the sense of God's intimacy was restored. It wasn't as though I suddenly felt there was a God hiding behind the olive tree. There wasn't someone around that I'd not noticed. It's more like discovering a hidden depth within oneself. Because God isn't another person. God is the deepest interior of oneself.

The eternal challenge to Christianity is the suffering in the world. Why does God allow such suffering?

Because God is not the big boss. He's not Prime Minister of the world. A God who is always tinkering would in the end be a very small sort of God.

But is he all-powerful?

He's all-powerful, but ultimately his power is not to intervene. His power is the power of love to be with us in our suffering and to bring us beyond it. I think that when you encounter deep suffering, what shows you the power of God is the simple way sisters and brothers are there with the suffering, sharing the anguish and pointing beyond it.

Do you believe in an interventionist God, who could perform miracles?

Yes, I believe that miracles do happen. But I think the normal way that God is present is by being at the heart of our lives.

It seems a very harsh perspective to take if that's how God operates.

I think that faced with suffering, you could try and argue it away. You could try and explain it, and sometimes we do that. But if you're faced with somebody who's suffering you don't start producing theological arguments. The people who I think can carry conviction at that point are those Christians who are themselves suffering.

I wonder if that isn't a way of avoiding the question.

I think it's a way of sharing the answer.

❖

9

DAVID PUTTNAM

'Film allows you insights into your own ethical being'

David Puttnam has been Britain's leading film producer for some three decades. After 10 years in advertising he launched a career that includes such award-winning films as Bugsy Malone, Midnight Express, Local Hero, The Mission, The Killing Fields, Chariots of Fire *and* Memphis Belle. *From 1986 to 1988 he was Chair and Chief Executive of Columbia Pictures – the only non-American to run a Hollywood Studio. He retired from film production in 1998 and throughout the Blair years has focused his career on education: in 2000 he was first Chair of the General Teaching Council and founding Chair of the National Endowment for Science, Technology and the Arts. In 2002 he was appointed President of Unicef UK. He was appointed to the House of Lords in 1997.*

Film, uniquely, has the ability to allow you insights into the workings of your ethical instincts. It allows you the conceit of imagining yourself a hero or even a martyr. It allows you the conceit of standing up for the principles, the things you believe in irrespective of the pain and ghastliness that it may cost you. So it offers the opportunity to inspire and encourage you towards being the very best you can.

But it also carries with it the risk of being the reverse of that?

Absolutely, and that's all in the hands of the film makers. I spent most of my career urging film makers to understand the extraordinary opportunity the medium gives them and not to indulge themselves or take advantage of the audience by using the negative potential of the medium. To allow people to as it were escape into the fantasies which are in themselves sometimes quite dangerous. The kind of role models that I saw as a young man in the cinema and that I formulated for myself were both people and incidents which allowed me to see myself as something better. I was very conscious as a young man of my inadequacies. Cinema allowed me the conceit of believing that I was better than that.

Your father was a very strong influence on your life. Tell me something about him.

He was a photo-journalist with Associated Press for many years. He had a marvellous war. He was official photographer to the King for a while. He lived in Italy and in Algeria. He was with Churchill for quite a long time so he had an extraordinary insight into the world. He travelled very widely. He was a wonderful person. I absolutely worshipped him and he had this extraordinary ability to reduce the most complex issues at the end of the day to what was fair. 'Fair' was the word that he used constantly.

What values did you derive from his attitude?

I admired his principles and his spirit. I admired his moral certainty, that you could come up with what was fair and reasonable in any given situation. As I get older, I can see there are situations he didn't have to deal with and that he was functioning in a somewhat simpler time. World War II was made for my dad. The issues were relatively black and white. And he was a strong man. I remember as a child when he came back from the war, getting into bed beside him, and cuddling up to him and this tremendous sense of strength and my little arm that would only go half way round his body, and thinking that this was the most wonderful rock.

Were his expectations of you very great, and did that put you under pressure? Did you feel the need to succeed?

I think he had quite specific dreams and hopes for me and he was quite helpful to me in the early part of my career. But no he didn't ever put me under any pressure. My mother similarly. And I realise that looking back to their reaction on my passing my Eleven-Plus – literally the family broke into a kind of hysterics – I remember waking up to the shriek of my mother pounding up the stairs and throwing herself on me, and being absolutely wild with delight. Obviously it had been a very, very big thing for them. They had probably been terribly concerned as to what they were going to do financially if I failed. Yet they hadn't passed that sense of anxiety on to me.

You won a place to a grammar school. Did you see it as a huge opportunity?

No, my entire academic career was a mystery to me. I ended up leaving school with four O levels. I certainly wasn't any kind of success. I simply 'existed' through my school years. I just wanted to get in and out of school as quietly and quickly as possible. My principal objective on any given day was not to be noticed. The important thing was just to get through it and not to make a fuss or cause problems. Whatever happened subsequently in my life was totally unrelated to what happened at school.

You certainly drew attention to yourself at Sunday school because you were expelled for setting off fireworks there. Was churchgoing part of the family life?

My parents took at a stab at it. I don't know how committed they were to it. My mother came from a Jewish background although she was brought up by her Protestant aunt so it was a mixed background. And, yes, I let some jumping crackers off during Sunday school.

But did you take it seriously as well?

Well, a very strange thing happened. My first year at grammar school I came top in RI and the pain and misery that caused me from my peers was so intense that I made damn sure it never, ever happened again. It was just the case that I'd read a lot about St Paul in the *Eagle* comic, I had a good memory and all the questions were about St Paul. I ended up with around 97 per cent and I just remembered the screams and howls of derision when the results were read out. I swore I'd never do it again.

Is St Paul still a hero?

St Paul was and remains a puzzle to me. I think he was a difficult man. I like his way with words but I suspect I would have thoroughly disliked him as a person. I would have got on better with Jesus!

If your school didn't make an impact, cinema certainly did. You refer to cinema as your education.

Yes it was. I engaged with cinema every bit as much as I avoided school. I'd certainly go to the cinema twice a week, sometimes three times.

And the films you cite as being important to you are the ones that have a moral underpinning. A Man For All Seasons *for example.*

Yes, *A Man for all Seasons* was, if you like, the begetter of *Chariots of Fire*. I spent all the years after seeing *A Man For All Seasons* trying to find a story that I felt could have similar resonance, and in a funny way if you look at the two films together they do. They're wholly dissimilar in one respect but they have quite broad similarities.

What was it about A Man for All Seasons? *An uncompromising man, Sir Thomas More: he's a saint now but at the time he was a politically astute, quite dogmatic, uncompromising figure who clashed with the King. A shrewd politician, in fact. Does that appeal to the politician in you?*

That's an interesting point. I think there is a politician in me and I think it's the politician in me that was attracted to or understood what More was all about. I was attracted by the relationships, the family relationships and the fantastic moral argument. But most of all, I used the word earlier and I mean it, it was the conceit of believing that I myself could stand up for something and believe in something so much that I'd go to my death for it. And I think that's a very important thing, I remember crying my eyes out at the end of *A Tale of Two Cities*, absolutely crying my eyes out, for the same reason.

That there was something worth dying for?

Yes. One of the things that has been most important to me I think in recent years has been the death of my best friend Terence Donovan, who was a wonderful man and very important in my life. And he committed suicide and I've pondered it a lot and I think I understand it. Terry was someone who'd had a wonderful life for 60 years and the future looked much more bleak than the past and he just decided not to deal with it. He never was a compromiser, he couldn't compromise, he was incapable of compromise.

So is the uncompromising nature of people's decisions something you admire? Another film you cite is Stanley Kramer's Inherit the Wind. *That's about the teacher who is teaching Darwinism in the southern States and stood accused in court.*

It was the first time I'd ever been confronted with two opposing views of a complex moral issue. And I was riveted by the fact that these two titans clashed over these issues, and did it in the way that they did. I was also very moved by the very end when Spencer Tracy, being congratulated on having as it were destroyed Fredric March's position, makes it clear that March's moral certainty may have been wrong-headed, but that it had a strength and commitment that he himself lacked. I was very touched by that.

You were living this rich interior life of the imagination that the cinema nurtured, but living in a small, modest home in north London. How are the two to be matched?

Well you must remember that my father because of his job was a window into another, bigger world. I remember sitting one evening, I guess it would have been 1948 so I'd have been seven and the news, the radio news came over that Count Bernadotte had been shot in Palestine and watching my father weep. And I always remember what he said, he said 'Those bloody fools, they've killed the best friend they ever had.' And Bernadotte was this early UN negotiator seeking a solution to the Palestinian problem. So, as I say, I had a window into another world.

And yet you went into advertising. Advertising is raw competition: people are eager to get on, they're in competition with other agencies, they're in competition with products, they're out to capture the public by whatever means they can. How does this tally with these high ideals?

First of all the job said 'boy wanted' – it sounded better than insurance and a lot better than banking. It was advertising and I was a messenger. And I did well. I liked it. It was my university in a sense. The third agency I worked for was Collett Dickinson Pierce. It had just started and I worked with a group of an extraordinary people. Charles Saatchi, Alan Parker. In hindsight it was a crash course in reality. You take this kind of dazed kid aged 17, leaving school earlier than he was supposed to and going into this other world of blistering reality. I think if I'd gone into something more idealistic when I was 17, I shudder to think where I'd have ended up!

Now as for your films, you have reservations about one of your very earliest successes, Midnight Express *– a story of drugs in Turkey and a very violent film. What are your reservations?*

It was a real wake-up call to me. I suddenly realised what the power of cinema was. We thought that we had created a morally balanced film and we thought we knew what effect it would have on the audience. It wasn't until I saw the film actually with an audience in New York and they were on their feet cheering the violence. That's when I realised that I knew nothing. I'd better go back to square one. But interestingly enough I think *Chariots of Fire* was to an extent a reaction to that.

A priest, a Catholic priest, helped bring your ideas into focus. Can you tell me about that?

I was going through a difficult time and I became friendly

with a marvellous man called Father Jack Mahoney who'd been head of Heythrop College and we talked. He reminded me of the power of the cinema and he said 'Stop looking at it as a negative thing, start looking at it as a positive thing. Stop questioning that power. Start using it. Turn it into something that's positive.' And I think that the flow of films that began then, first with *Chariots of Fire*, and then following on with *Local Hero* and *The Mission*, *The Killing Fields* and *Cal* had a lot to do with those conversations I had with Jack.

Are you saying that you're using cinema to preach to people?

No, I hope not. I'm trying to use stories to illustrate the positive impact that people can have on each other – the power of friendship, the power of belief, the power of commitment because, as I said, cinema allows the audience the conceit of believing it could be about them. There's no question that the power of *Chariots of Fire* lies in the fact that the audience watching that film also decide they might refuse to run on a Sunday, and they feel good about it. And they get their reward for feeling good about it. So there's a marvellous sense of catharsis. You feel you've stood up for something, you've taken a stand, and you become rewarded.

Eric Liddell's decision not to run on a Sunday in Chariots of Fire *was because he was a very devout Christian and he didn't want to abuse the Lord's day. Do you feel that Sunday's a sacred day?*

No, I feel that the Europeans always understood it much better than us. Europeans use Sunday very well. They expect to go to church, they come out of church and have lunch with their families and then go to a football match or some other activity in the afternoon. I think that's a very productive and profitable way to spend a Sunday. There's a joy to it. I remember Sundays in the '50s in Britain were awful. People not only didn't go to church, they didn't do anything. They sat in front of their television sets and overate and slept through the afternoon. I don't think there's anything very religious about that.

How do you yourself spend Sunday now?

I go to church, but regular attendance has happened in only the last decade. Prior to that I used to go when we were in the country and that would have been every second or third week.

I go to an Anglo-Catholic church. I like the dignity of it and I like the tradition of it. I get a lot of reassurance by saying almost the same prayers every Sunday. There's one moment in the service that has always seemed to me to be the most important. It's the 'Blessed is He who comes in the name of the Lord'. I find it very moving and for me that's what that day what that hour is all about. My wife, Patsy and I only got confirmed in 1997 which was something I think we had wanted to do. For years I'd gone to church and watched other people go up to the altar rail to take communion. And now I feel much more comfortable about that.

Is the taking of communion very significant for you?

It's all of a piece with being there. I find going to church on a Sunday very strengthening. I bring my problems in, I meditate on them and I go out feeling stronger and better and firmer in my belief.

How would you define your God?

My God's benign. He's very much the God of the New Testament, not the Old Testament. I have a problem with the Old Testament in terms of its moral position. The God of the

115

New Testament is hopeful. He has the same attitude to us that I have towards to education in Britain which is that if we try hard enough we can make a go of it. It's very difficult. There are no simple answers. But you have to believe that the future's going to be better than the past. And I think that's what my God does.

In The Mission *you tell the story of the Jesuit rebels who defy the Catholic Church in Rome because of their commitment to the native peoples in South America. Institutionalised churches often present problems for their rebellious and assertive members. Have you found that to be so in your case?*

I've always had some problems with religious orthodoxy. You can't study history without seeing how many extraordinary errors the Church has made and how unbelievably cruel the Church has been. On the other hand there are many things about the Church which is absolutely, wholly admirable. My wife works a lot in a Leprosy Mission in India, north Bihar, in north-western India. And she works with Indian Catholic priests and she quite rightly says that these are the most extraordinary people she's ever met in her life. Their entire life is devoted to service. So through her I'm able to see how lives can be lived if you have enough of a sense of what you're on the earth for.

You made The Killing Fields *about the retreat of Americans from Cambodia. Again a great friendship between two men which features in many of your films and you showed appalling atrocity. The problem for believers in an interventionist God is why does God allow such suffering?*

Because he gave us the right of self-determination and he can't stop us. He can't stop us, he made the decision not to be able stop us behaving badly and what he does is, I think, throw his weight as much as possible on the scales of what the Church would call righteousness or what we might call truth, in the hope that truth will overcome. When you look at the twentieth century it's very puzzling, because on the one hand broadly speaking the good guys won, but the price that was paid and the death and destruction that occurred during that century in order for that to be the outcome is incomprehensible.

Do you think that evil is a positive force at large in the world?

I think evil is a positive force at large in all of us. I've always believed that the battle that rages inside us is just a miniature of the battle that rages in the world in general. I think that within us we all carry the seeds of our own destruction and of our own salvation.

You have said that creative artists have a moral responsibility to challenge, inspire, question and affirm. This is a powerfully crusading approach you're taking to life.

I don't think it is. To ask someone who has the God-given gifts to communicate or influence, to do it in a way which is ethical and positive and constructive and serves the purposes of society generally. I don't think that's asking a lot. It's just complete common sense.

When you look at the movies that get made now, the blockbusters, the violent movies, the exploitative movies, don't you ever doubt or despair?

I despair of the stupidity of the people making them. I mean I've always used the most simple rubric imaginable. Why would you make a film, the net effect of which could be to damage the society in which you and your family live?

For profit?

But that is still madness, to indulge in a profitable activity which damages the society that you live in. It's not as though you can escape from the society you live in, it's not as though you can go and live somewhere else. Why would you ever involve yourself for profit in something which damaged those you love and made their lives impoverished?

David, as you shape up the endgame of your life, do you feel that you're fulfilling some sort of destiny, some sort of purpose that has been planned for you by your God?

That's a really difficult question. The only way I can answer it is this: I feel that all of us have a destiny or maybe the opportunity of a destiny. What I'm trying to do is optimise the opportunity. I don't want to pop my clogs having felt that opportunities cinema, or more recently the world of education, have created for me, haven't been used to promote the world that my father would have believed in. You see, it comes back to my father. After World War II, he genuinely believed in 1945 when the Labour government came in, that the world had changed forever in the right direction. I would love to feel that part and parcel of what I'd done in my life had been to prove him right.

❖

10

JAMES MACMILLAN

'Inspiration has a divine dimension'

James Macmillan first came to the attention of the musical world as a prize-winner in the 1983 Norwich Festival of Contemporary Music. In the 21 years since then he has published over 120 works, many of them choral, and many of them using the Catholic liturgy and ideas rooted in his Catholicism, his Scottishness and his left-leaning politics. In 2000 became composer/conductor with the BBC Philharmonic in Manchester.

People do have a sense there's something sublime about music, don't they?

Well I certainly believe that music could be described very possibly as the most spiritual of the arts. Because music seems to touch something very deep within the human soul. It seems to get into those dark crevices in the relationship between the self and the divine. And lovers of music talk about their lives being transformed through the power of music in quasi-religious language. Music does have this effect on people, on individuals, that it brings about momentous changes in their lives in a way analogous to the impact of religion.

What is it that allows music to do that?

This is the great mystery of music – what is music? Is music the notes on the page? Is music the sound that we hear? In that case you can't touch it, you can't hold it, you can't kiss it, you can't eat it. It's this strange intangible thing that is not material and is not even visible but yet has this overwhelming, sometimes convulsive effect on human beings. In many ways it touches the analogy with the divine because people talk about God or the divine having those kind of qualities. They're invisible but yet palpable.

Do you think of music as having a moral force?

I do. I'm encouraged by a whole range of composers throughout history and in our own time who have hinted in their work and in their words that this is indeed the case. And I'm especially intrigued by the likes of Shostakovich who talked in terms of the moral potential of art and especially music. And here was this very public atheist at least making some statements in his work and about his work and about art generally which points to something deeper in the implication of art and music. That music may indeed have a power to direct our concerns, our social, political and religious concerns. And then of course there are many composers throughout history who have – and I'm thinking of particular composers like Beethoven – who have been great inspirations precisely because they hinted at the extra-musical dimension of music.

You've always been very up-front about your Catholic faith. Was it simply spontaneous? Has it been built into you from very early childhood?

There was certainly a time as a younger man that I worried a little bit about the Catholicism being so public. But I came to a realisation that the work was so informed and so infused by many things, extra-musical things, Catholicism being the most important, that I couldn't really hide it any more and there was no point in playing games with people.

So what kind of childhood was it? Sunday school, church on Sundays, confession?

Yes, I grew up in the west of Scotland. I would say my parents were liberal Catholics. It was a happy practising devout Catholic community, a little bit insular perhaps and a little bit wary of the majority non-Catholic community. I think that's the way of the west-coast Scottish Catholic community. But nevertheless a community that mediated the ideas to each other through their own personal histories and through a very particular culture. Mass attendance was important, I was an altar boy, I was taught by nuns of the Sacred Heart order.

James Joyce's Portrait of the Artist as a Young Man *tells his account of how being a child in a Catholic home put him off his Catholic faith but this clearly didn't happen to you. It reinforced you.*

I was a young Catholic in the '60s when Vatican II was beginning to bring about many, many changes and these were changes that were wanted by the community I was in. I remember by parents were idealistic and happy young Catholics in the 1960s and they saw the influence of Vatican II and the influence of people like John XXIII as indication of a better world. That they were heading in a positive direction. That's the kind of Catholicism that I grew up in and I'm glad of that.

You had a very important teacher, Herbert Richardson, in your life. Was it he who put you on the path to music?

In many ways that's right. He and I became friends when I was a teenager. I had already embarked on a life of music and

I knew at a very early stage that I wanted to be a musician. I even knew within weeks of beginning music that I wanted to be a composer, although I didn't know what it really meant as early as that. But then to encounter the great encouragement and joy in music, joy in life in the character of Herbert Richardson was a great inspiration, a compounding factor on the way that things developed after that.

People speak of gifted children and presumably you think of yourself as having been given the gift of music. Who gave it to you? Some people might say it was a gift from God.

Yes, it's an area I'm very wary of treading because it can look rather glib. I think that gifts, talking about it theologically, are given to many people and it's just getting the right fertile ground for those gifts to blossom that is probably more important and that's why I'm passionate about being able to encourage gifts in other people in the way that Herbert Richardson encouraged me. I think if one is gifted in that way then one has to reflect it back to our peers, to our community in some way and that's what I admire about the likes of Maxwell Davies because he sees his role not just as being a composer but to encourage gifts that are there, that he knows are there in other people.

So you see your music carrying responsibilities with it?

I would like to think that that is the case. I do believe that composers and artists are in many ways channels of something, something objective, something divine, that inspiration has a divine dimension and that, because music does have this hugely transformative impact on individuals and has been proven to be that way, then there is a responsibility on the composer to channel back divine truths to our society, to our peers.

Now let's consider another side of your personality. In your adolescence you joined the Young Communist League. How did you manage to match the two ideologies?

I was very aware of the contradiction between these two credos. Certainly when I took that step to join the Communist Party, I was opposed by people within my community including some well-meaning family members, not my parents I hasten to add, who were very interested if a little wary of the path I was taking. But I was very aware of not just the contradiction between the two ideas, or ideologies, but in many ways the parallel between them, a fascinating parallel, a fascinating grey area sometimes that brought the two together. It was clear to me that the attractive, idealistic and ideological thirst for justice on the left had its roots in the words of Jesus and what he had to say about the poor and the dispossessed and the prisoner and so on. And even though I wasn't aware of it then, I suppose I've been involved ever since in probing the parallel between a left-wing idealism and the idealism of the Gospel. So for me it wasn't a case of turning my back on one ideology and flirting with another. It was probing the differences and the similarities of both which has proved a fascinating lifelong journey for me.

Presumably this made you critical in some ways of the wealth of the Church, the power of the Church, the authority of the Church?

All of those things and also of the Church's ability to traduce the fundamental message. I think that for most Catholics who decide to leave the Church for political or ideological or idealistic reasons that is the big stumbling block, the fact that the Church's role throughout history has in many ways been a betrayal of those fundamental impulses of goodness, those fundamental messages of justice and peace.

Is that what drew you to the radical liberation theology in Latin America?

I think it was one contemporary way of exploring the perpetual parallelism between the two ideologies. I remember going along to conferences of the Young Communist League when I was 14, 15 and missing out the Sunday morning session to go to mass and that caused great consternation amongst my new-found comrades in ways parallel to the consternation that had been caused in my family community back home. But one reason that I've decided to stick with it is that I look at the experience of say the first Pope, St Peter and I see very human failings that I can recognise in him and the fact that he was given authority points to something I think in the thinking of God. That God so loved the world that he was willing to put up with the traducing, the betrayal that would happen over the next 2000 years and forgive us for that. I mean the Catholic Church has been in crisis since St Peter heard the cock crow, and I think always will be. But as long as that crisis is provoking thought and self-examination I think that the Church is probably still taking the right line.

Tell me about the influence of the Dominicans whom you knew when you were a student.

There was something about the Dominican ethos as a student, a young student Catholic that proved to be very influential. The Dominicans set up a series of talks at Edinburgh called 'Objections to Catholicism' and they used to invite a series of speakers in who would give us a very, very hard time from one perspective or another. Sometimes they would be Marxists, sometimes humanists, secularists, sometimes extreme Protestants. And they would outline a whole series of objections to the faith to which we had to respond and more importantly think. And to be able to subject our own faith to that kind of close scrutiny from others and then from ourselves I think is a great favour you can do to any young enquiring Catholic mind.

How much have you been able to use your music and your composi-tions to address directly political issues of this kind?

That's a very hard question because music, as well as being one of the most spiritual of the arts, is also at a fundamental level the most abstract of the arts. And musicians and compos-ers take a pride in the fact that music at a fundamental level doesn't need any justification or point to it other than its own substance, its own musical technique and being. Therefore on that definition, music is not a political thing at all, but music in collaboration with the other arts and especially with literature and with words can provide a moral and political impetus and I've certainly been aware of that. And I also believe that music should never become a mere loudhailer for any cause or creed. You can hear music demeaning itself when it simply sees no further than a political cause. Having said that, in our own age composers have wanted to allow their music to be a channel for these things and I have in certain circumstances seen the potential for that, for example in a work called *Busqueda*, which is a setting of poems by the Mothers of the Disap-peared from Argentina. It allowed me to probe again the parallels between religion and politics, between the sacred and the secular, and I think that has an impact though these kind of works, like the *War Requiem* by Benjamin Britten or *A Child of Our Time* by Michael Tippett or even for that matter *Fidelio* by Beethoven – all of which have an impact beyond the notes on the page.

I'm interested in the selection you make of texts. From the liturgy, you use the Lord's Prayer in Aramaic, you use texts from the Catholic liturgy, you use the Seven Last Words from the Cross.

I think the great Crucifixion and Resurrection narrative is something that is so much at the core of our society, whether you accept its veracity or not, it's there, it's a given in our society. I'm attracted to them because of my own personal but mediated faith. I've been given the gift of this tradition through people I've known, through teachers, through parents, through tradition, through the communion of the saints, through the Fathers of the Church, through the Gospels. I do believe there's a divine element but it's mediated to us through all these other things. And I feel compelled, driven to respond to that gift by engaging with these great texts, by this great story, by dealing with the crucifixion narrative, by circling round it rather obsessively perhaps, in many different works. But there's a great reservoir and a great depth of inspiration in these texts for me.

When you're working on such a text your spiritual life must be very much in the foreground of a large part of your daily life, which is unusual for most people.

I think you're right. Most people do not encounter silence on that daily basis, on that regular basis. And for that I feel myself truly fortunate that in order to be me, in order to be the composer I want to be I need that solace and silence. If I was not a religious person, I would still be encountering a silence which would be analogous to the world of prayer or the context of prayer. But because I'm religious and see the analogies and the connections only too clearly and too deeply, in the silence of the imagination, the truly necessary silence where music must begin, there is also this deep connection between the self and the divine which is explored through prayer on a daily basis.

It can be difficult sometimes. My children know not to disturb me. But I do believe that music cannot exist in a vacuum and that musical inspiration does not happen in a vacuum separate from real life. I think that true spirituality grows out of the truly corporeal, the everyday, the mundane even, but also the ordinary recognisable joys and sorrows that are common to all of us, the grit and mire of daily life, the sense of sadness and the abyss as well as joy and transcendence.

You said when you were nearing 40 you were suddenly aware of a darkening of your musical output. Was it a darkening of your personal mood as well?

Not on a deeply personal level. I have a very happy life, a happy family life. I feel greatly blessed by having my three children and Lynn my wife. But a shadow has passed over the music and those senses of silence in ways that I cannot yet account for. I wouldn't say it's a purely private psychological thing. Perhaps it comes from this need to engage with the world. I don't see my music existing in a vacuum, some little aesthetic corner siphoned off from the rest of human experience. I regard myself as a fully paid up member of society with my roots firmly in a communitarian sense of what the human race is and an awareness, indeed a love of humanity.

I wonder whether the shadow comes from a problem for all people who believe in an interventionist God, which is the problem that suffering poses for believers.

Yes, I suppose that gets directly to the daily struggle of one's faith. What is the purpose of suffering? And if one cannot make any sense of it at all it can have a devastating effect spiritually, it can make one become apostate. It can make one fall away from any sense of a loving God. And for faith to remain alive it has continually to be probed by these uncomfortable questions and I think these questions are valid and I especially think this one is.

You probe, but what do you find?

Well I think that there is sometimes a very thin dividing line between having a faith and not having a faith and many people cross that dividing line quite regularly with great suffering in their own selves. That's why I do not feel too distant from those who say they do not have faith, because I sometimes feel that that dividing line is very, very thin and that perhaps people have crossed that divide once too often to be on one side or the other.

You set a great many texts of the liturgy and you referred earlier to Pope John and Vatican II. I wonder how you feel with your huge regard for church music, for the tradition of church music, about the relatively new practices in Catholic churches, the lay involvement and the vernacular. How do you feel about that? Is that all gain?

Mostly gain I would say. I think many right-wing Catholics look back on pre-Vatican II days with rather rose-tinted spectacles. The liturgy was not always beautiful then in Latin. The liturgies could be rather dreary, alienating affairs. And the Church needed to open its arms again and embrace the people that were being kept well back from the divine mysteries. But there seems to be a flight from beauty in a lot of the liturgy and a sense that the most practical, the most prosaic music will do. That's something that worries me a little a bit.

Do you see your beliefs changing and developing or are they fundamentally consistent and rooted and unchanging?

I would say that they are rooted and always changing and I think that's the way that a Catholic faith has to be. It wouldn't be Catholic if it was not rooted in a tradition in the sense of the communion of the saints and what the Fathers of the Church have given us. And what the Apostles who knew Christ have given us. In a sense if being a Catholic means an acknowledgement of the fact that faith is mediated to us through all of this, that faith is more than just the privatised relationship, the personal relationship between oneself and God. If that's what being a Catholic means then count me in, but it must continually be probed as society develops and as history progresses so that the faith must always be like a kaleidoscope changing and becoming more suited to history as it moves forward. But to lose roots makes one aimless as we approach the future.

✻

11

AMY TAN

'A spiritual meditation'

The American novelist, Amy Tan, is the daughter of Chinese immigrants and she draws on their background and personalities for her novels, most notably The Joy Luck Club, *published in 1989 which was an instant best seller and subsequently made into a film. Others have followed:* The Kitchen God's Wife *in 1991,* The Hundred Secret Senses *in 1998, and* The Bonesetter's Daughter *in 2001. Her first work on non-fiction,* The Opposite of Fate, *examines her inheritance from her highly individual family, and the traumas of their life and death.*

My mother was the person who determined my perception of the world, as any mother would be for a daughter. To her the world was a malevolent place. I remember very early on her telling me for example that she might die, and whether she would die would depend on my behaviour. She would suggest that she might kill herself if things didn't go the way that she had hoped. She had an eclectic range of beliefs that came from different religions. One was of course Buddhism and the other Ancestor Worship. Some things were based on animism, which I suppose Westerners would call superstition. She had been raised in a Catholic boarding school so she had some experience of Western theology. But she also had a belief in ghosts. My father was a Baptist minister so she kept that hidden from him for the most part because the only ghost that was allowed in the house was the Holy Ghost. And her comments about ghosts would have been blasphemous.

Did she pass any of these ideas on to you?

Her belief was that she could look for answers in all places, she was the ultimate pragmatist. She could look for miracles, she could look for curses, she could look for beliefs in an afterlife, she could look at heaven as a possibility for reward. And they were all there and they sort of co-existed in a way, rather mutually, without seeming contradiction for her.

But then there was her most extraordinary temperament, which of course you've used in many of your novels. One of the most extraordinary characters, if I can use such a word, that I've ever encountered.

She also had a very passionate temperament and she was the most hopeful person. I realised looking back she was somebody who would go to all extremes of hope and yet she was also filled with more sorrow and despair, unrelenting sorrow about things that had happened to her. She believed that all men contained within them the potential to destroy your life and she was constantly warning me about that with my relationships. Some of it came out early when I was young, and I knew nothing about relationships with men. Her idea of sex education was to say 'Don't let a boy kiss you because if you do you will have a baby, then you'll put the baby in a garbage can, the police will come and arrest you and take you to jail and you might as well kill yourself.'

Have you struggled to throw off this legacy that you had from her?

I tried to remove as much influence as possible but it's impossible. You are shaped by your parents, whether you rebel against that or not. Some of the things you rebel against then become simply a reactive stance. The rest I think just seep insidiously into my personality, my own beliefs and my character. I think of myself however as a very optimistic person; I'm very hopeful but not with the same sense of foreboding that my mother had.

The opposite of fate in fact?

The opposite of fate and being able to create a different answer. Sometimes in childhood, I found opportunities to change fate. My mother believed that I could talk to ghosts through an Ouija board. I knew of course that I was coming up with the answers by pushing the planchet. So when my mother would say things to me like 'Oh Amy treat me so bad, what I should do is send her to school for bad girls.' And then I just scooted over to the 'no' answer and in that way, changed that particular fate that my mother might have had in mind for me. I think of writing as being a way to change fate, which really is changing in essence the perception of your life and the direction it's taking, and also the direction it's gone, the direction your family history has gone.

Is that why you don't want to resolve completely all the legacy of conflicts and distress because it fuels your writing?

Oh yes, absolutely. It's the questions that really fuel my writing. The very simple questions a child asks, 'How do things happen?', 'Who makes things happen?', 'How do I make things happen?' And that evolved into adulthood and as a fiction writer into stories in which I recall things from my

132

childhood. But I also infuse imagination in a narrative that's fictional, that creates one possible answer to those questions. I think of fiction as being a narrative, which takes all this chaos in the world and puts it into a fashion that is its own cosmology. Every story contains some element of belief about how the world works. Whether it's a belief in fate or accidents or luck or destiny or simply self-determination.

Now your father, a Baptist minister, died of a brain tumour when you were 15 years old. What influence did he have on you?

I didn't question his beliefs in childhood. They were just so much a part of our life from the beginning, the quality of his faith was part of our family. We prayed at every meal, we asked for God's guidance, there were certain rules of behaviour that we followed; no drinking, no swearing. A belief that one had to accept Jesus Christ as one's personal saviour in order to go to heaven and that those who didn't do that would go to hell. Beliefs that you had to subscribe to and very much a life with prescribed behaviours. I didn't question it until one of my father's beliefs – that absolute faith could work miracles, and that my brother, who was stricken with a brain tumour at age 16, would somehow recover. And instead of my brother recovering, my father was also stricken with a brain tumour a month before my brother died. And I kept thinking that somehow the miracle would still happen. When it didn't I became an angry person who discarded all my father's beliefs, all the religious beliefs, because I couldn't trust him anymore.

Do you think he lost his faith at the end of his life?

I don't really know. At the end of his life his brother came to him and said that this had occurred in our family – the brain tumour of both my father and my brother – because my father had married my mother, a woman who was a divorcee. And this was God's will, his punishment upon our family for this transgression.

The punishing God is a very damaging thing isn't it?

It was a malevolent religion and I wanted to reject that completely. I was a very angry teenager at the time and so I took those very strict beliefs and not only rebelled against them but decided that I was rebelling against any kind of hope in the world.

You had a bad experience after your father's death when an elder of the Church molested you.

Yes I think it contributed to my loss of faith because I found that the people I had most trusted were no longer trustworthy and in fact were evil. I saw minor things such as a person smoking or drinking wine and that of course made me rather cynical. But this person who was a member of the Church, had molested me. It was so shocking and yet I couldn't say anything because my mother would become upset.

Now the contrast between this very clear-cut Baptist Christianity and your mother's chaotic mix of ideas, did this create tension as you were trying to sort out what life was about?

It did create tension within me and for a while a desire to reject everything, to reject anything positive, anything hopeful. It made me angry for example that my mother would not give up on my father at the end: she was calling in faith healers who spoke in tongues; she was beseeching the doctors to try new chemotherapies; she asked a geomancer to come in the house and inspect the spiritual architecture, to determine if forces were aligned against us.

And in fact one of the means of dealing with all of this was to move us to Europe. She found within the house a sign, and that was a can that said something like 'Old Dutch cleanser'. It was a cleanser that you used to clean sinks. And she looked at it and said 'Holland is clean, we should move to Holland.' And a few months later we actually boarded the SS *Rotterdam* and we sailed to Holland. I mean this is unbelievable and I look at myself now and I'm about the same age my mother was at the time and I can't imagine my doing this with two young, angry teenagers, going to a land where I know nothing. I know nothing about the country itself or the language or anyone who lives there. And that's what she did to get away from this curse.

And then on your 24th birthday your close friend Peter was murdered violently and you had to identify his body. And that had a profound influence on you.

Well Pete was somebody who believed in things that you would consider transcendental. He liked to ask questions about the universe, about immortality, eternity. And he would say things like 'Are these things predestined or are we following a path, or do we create the path ourselves?' And these questions didn't become important to me until after he died and I realised that in effect what happened was that I inherited his questions. You inherit things when people die and they are not just material possessions, they are the questions that they asked and you have to go on to find the answers. I began to look for these by taking on a life that I thought was in a more worthwhile direction, and that was to work with children with disabilities.

Did his death lead you to change your view of life after death?

In the beginning it certainly did because I wanted to believe that he continued in life in some form. In fact he was coming to me in dreams and helping me to resolve a lot of the issues I had about my own self-esteem and inadequacies. They would be dreams about me learning to fly for the first time with a pair of plastic wings and when I suddenly realised that they were plastic I would tumble and almost fall and be killed. Eventually I learned that it was my belief that I could fly that enabled me to do that and not the plastic wings. And that was the lesson, that I didn't need the props anymore and I really should go out and believe in myself and do the things that were important. And I leave it very open. Whether there are spirits in some form I'm not exactly sure. I wouldn't call them ghosts, ghosts is a very pejorative term. But I have a sense of the spirit, the sense of the soul. We don't know how that continues after life, or whether it continues. I prefer to believe that it does and that it's in the form of whatever we call the essence of love. This quality that love is actually something that you cannot define implicitly, you can't see implicit evidence or explicit evidence. It's all something we sense, we feel, just as we sense ghosts or we sense the spirit, we sense so much that is considered religious experience, spiritual experience. And that love is the feeling that I feel most when I've had occurrences of what people would call the supernatural.

After your father's death you spoke of losing your Christian faith.

What I really lost was the idea of a set of beliefs handed to me. What I look for now are spiritual beliefs. Beliefs that are based on questions not only about life after death but also about our purpose in life. I think that religion and spirituality are also concerned with those questions, 'What is the meaning of life, what is our purpose as human beings, during our existence, and how is our belief in an afterlife shaping what we do?' And those are questions that I ask when I'm writing. I think of writing as a meditation, a spiritual meditation on the most important questions in life and that in devising fictional stories I'm answering that in some way. I'm creating a cosmology, a theology even about what happens, whether our lives are governed by luck or chance or choice or self-determination.

But you don't feel that we're just buffeted around in some completely random universe?

No I don't believe in the random universe, I believe in human intentions and responsibilities and consequences. I also believe that there is a whole concatenation of things that happen in our life, based on many elements coming together at the same time. Some of which we cannot explain, we cannot find empirical evidence for isolating how that occurs. But certainly human will and determination and an attitude about life shapes that direction.

Was writing waiting for you as a vocation?

I think it had become an absolute necessity for me. When I found fiction writing, by then it was my reason for living. I hadn't been able to find it in work and that's why I had worked so hard, thinking the more I worked the more satisfaction and happiness I would find. And yet, though I was successful, it wasn't satisfying for me and I needed to find something I was passionate about. I could be passionate about my relationship with my husband but I had to be passionate about something else within my own self, my own life. Then once I found that it was as though it had been there all along, it was amazing to me; it had been there all along because it was in me. And yet now here was this perfect way to continue this thinking about my life and incorporating imagination, to answer these questions. I knew at that point, when I started to write fiction that I wouldn't ever give it up, even if nothing ever came of it.

But of course you did have an immediate success with The Joy Luck Club. *That kind of success rockets you into an entirely different orbit, or way of life, the attitude of the media towards you, other writers towards your success and so on. Was that critical for you?*

I was not expecting any of that and I was in fact frightened by it. I didn't know what to do with it. So I tried to believe that it was a fluke and that it would stop after about six weeks. And when it was still there six weeks later I said 'It'll stop in another month.' And it continued until I finally had to accept it. But I remember I cried the first day of publication, not knowing what was going to happen. It took me probably a year to adjust to the fact that my life had changed. And people began to look at me differently and expect that I would have answers to everything from human rights in China to global warming. My whole identity was called into question and I had to really focus on what I believed my identity was, as a writer, as a person, as a woman, as a Chinese American.

The books that followed – The Kitchen God's Wife, The Hundred Secret Senses *and* The Bonesetter's Daughter – *have nursed an interest and revelation of your background in different ways. That focussing on your background must have held your beliefs firm as well.*

What was important was to delve into those questions of how my past had shaped me and so necessarily how my mother had shaped me and how her mother had shaped her and so on. My interest in China is therefore prior to 1949, because my mother came to the United States in '49 and it was that history that I was more interested in, than say the China of today.

In The Bone Setter's Daughter *you draw on your mother's experience of getting Alzheimer's disease. Most people fear this terrible disease striking someone they love, because they feel it will alienate the relationship. You found the opposite didn't you?*

Yes, her memories changed and in part became happier ones. She seemed to forget about the losses that had plagued her and tormented her. And instead she found herself dwelling in the happier times, even the funny times. Now she saw them from a different light, almost with a sense of pride, that she had survived. She recalled that I had been there when she met my father. She said that I had taken her by elevator to a dance hall and that the elevator doors opened and that there my father was. And I told her to go off and dance with him and then I retreated into the elevator and she said 'Oh you were so sneaky.' She was so happy that I had done that. And I thought it was so wonderful that she had placed me in one of the happiest days of her life. How could I feel devastated by that? Though she had lost her memory and this was the memory of someone who had dementia, it was such a loving memory. A memory that said 'Here are two people I have loved the most in my life and I put them together at the same time, during this meeting.' She had other wonderful things that happened that were like a gift to me, a final gift. I was learning the emotion of what it's like to lose somebody so important. And that was very sad but also very necessary for us as human beings to experience the depth of that loss. I was learning that families are a necessary part of our becoming humans, because they test us in the absolute range of both love and of hate and despair and hope; all of those things.

In the years since then you yourself have been suffering from Lyme Disease. Has that experience also given your outlook on life a different perspective?

I was most distressed when I didn't know what it was. For a while I considered the curse that my mother had believed about the brain tumours – my father had one, my brother had one; my mother even had one, a benign brain tumour. And here I thought 'Well maybe I have the fourth brain tumour.' For four years we didn't really know what was going on. So when I got my diagnosis I instantly felt more hopeful about the possibilities of getting a cure. I've since found out that it's very hard to be cured completely if you've had this for a very long time. If you catch it early and you're treated properly then yes, you can get a total cure but I'm facing some difficulties possibly for the rest of my life. And yet I feel very blessed, I feel I can do something with this disease that's positive and so I've been doing some public awareness about Lyme Disease prevention, early diagnosis, treatment, but raising money to provide funds for children who have Lyme Disease whose parents cannot afford medical treatment. I think one takes some bit of turmoil in life and then tries to not just simply deal with it but take control. I could have just as easily said 'Well I'm a victim, I'm going to suffer, I'm very angry that the doctors didn't diagnose me, I'm going to try and sue them.' But I don't want to do that, I would rather do something positive. That's how I focus my life.

The role of the writer in American society is a highly-regarded one. It's almost as if writers have a priestly function, they're looked to for a moral leadership of some kind. Do you see yourself in those terms?

I think the writer has dualistic responsibilities. One is the responsibility to oneself and your own morality, your own sense of ethics. I think every literary writer is somehow grappling with their own morality. At the same time you are cognisant of the fact that your work is going to be read and interpreted and yet you can't have the total responsibility of the way that people think. Your work may be misinterpreted once it falls into the hands of another reader. Their own experiences and beliefs are going to intersect with your work and then the book becomes its own thing. I also believe that writers cannot create works that answer all the moral questions. Or if they attempt to, what happens is that the work descends into propaganda or diatribe of the worst type. And then you are no longer writing fiction. There is an art to it and part of it is that you are honest with yourself as a writer. You tell the truth only as you know it.

❋

12

ROBERT WINSTON

'Playing God …
the highest thing we can do'

Professor Robert Winston is a scientist, a world pioneer in the treatment of infertility. His work deals with potential life in a Petri dish, intervening as a scientist in the business of creating new life. He is Professor of Fertility Studies at Imperial College, London and Director of the NHS Research and Development Department of the Hammersmith Hospital. He is also a leading BBC broadcaster whose television series include The Human Body, The Secret Life of Twins, Superhuman *and* The Human Mind. *He is also a practising Orthodox Jew. Since 1995 he has been a member of the UK's second chamber, the House of Lords.*

Have you ever thought there was a conflict between science and religion?

I don't actually think there really is a conflict. At one important level, it seems to me that they are essentially both about the same thing. There's a notion that science is about black and white, about certainty, about absolute knowledge, about facts. The truth is that science really is about uncertainty, and I think that religion is also about uncertainty. I think that the two are very similar and I think they both portray some very similar facets. For example, in religion one of the reasons why people often have faith is because actually they aren't certain, and maybe certainty in religion is almost one of the worst things to have and maybe that's caused a huge amount of damage. With regard to uncertainty in science, there's no question that certainty in science has caused damage. Where there is a difference between science and religion is in the area of moral values. One of the things I often say, which seems to shock people for some reason that I don't understand, is that I believe very firmly that science itself does not have a moral dimension, it's the application of that science and the way you gain that knowledge that has the moral dimension.

What about the purpose of discovering more, the purpose of science, which may or not prove damaging to the human race?

Well, the truth is that if you're trying to gain knowledge, if it's pure knowledge, then of course you have no idea how it's going to be applied and you can't know beforehand what use it might be. The whole point about 'Blue Skies' research, of course, is exactly that. It's perfectly true that had we not got into nuclear physics, we wouldn't have made an atom bomb, but had we not understood the nature of radiation we wouldn't have X-rays either, which of course save far more lives than have been destroyed by nuclear physics.

Let's explore then your background. Your grandfather was a rabbi. How significant is such a legacy?

I think very significant. Recently for a television programme I was making I had my DNA traced by a genealogist, and he was able to show that I'd come from the Middle East. We'd gone through North Africa, we'd arrived in Spain. My family were in Spain in 1490, were expelled in 1492 and then went back to the Middle East, where in about 1700 some came to England via Amsterdam. What's interesting I think about those Sephardi families – those people who come from the Spanish-Portuguese tradition – is that by and large many of them have become assimilated because they've been in the United Kingdom for a long time. My family has remained quite Orthodox really, and there have been quite a number who have been rabbis, or if not rabbis, scholars, which is rather similar because a rabbi essentially is a scholar.

You give the impression of being steeped in an identity that goes back several hundred years.

But I think Jews are. That's one of the things about Judaism. There've been many times in my life when I've been totally irreligious, I mean completely non-conforming to any kind of religious view, doing things which would be widely condemned by Judaism, not keeping any of the dietary laws, not keeping any kind of laws, trying to find my own moral values. But I was always conscious that at the back of me was a very thorough tradition which I really valued. One of the great things about Judaism for me is the intellectual tradition. Judaism has a great respect for intellect, for human intelligence; it believes that human intelligence is God given and we should be using it … that's why we support science. Jews firmly believe in science as being an important tool because it's one of the tools of creation, and not to use science, not to explore with our intelligence is regarded as almost a defect.

Your father died when you were nine years old, so the sense of loss must have been enormously powerful.

Yes, I think it was. I was the oldest child so quite a lot fell on me. My mother, a highly intelligent, very powerful lady was not exactly destitute, but my father was, just like myself, a dreadful person at spending money. He wasn't very religious. It was essentially my mother's side that were much more religious.

Now you are part of the scientific community which has revealed to us that we are shaped by our genes and that genetic influence is very powerful. In a religious context we like to believe in free will. How much of your behaviour and your decisions in life are genetic and how much is free will?

I think what has been unfortunate, particularly since the announcement of the sequencing of the human genome, is the notion that we are totally determined by our genes. There is this creeping determinism which I think is actually quite damaging ... I think it's fundamentally flawed. It seems to me that there is a risk about being deterministic. But when you look at genetics, what you are constantly struck by is that the environment has a very powerful influence.

None the less, from what you know of genetics, you speak of your spendthrift father and your rather serious-minded religious mother, do you recognise these impulses in you, whether they're genetic or not?

I think I probably got the wrong genes from both parents. Consequently, I'm rather spendthrift and much too argumentative.

People outside that faith see it as a matter of observances. How strictly do you observe the rules of Judaism?

I think you're right to touch on observance because, although we pray about our faith and talk about how the Messiah will come, has not yet come, the truth is that many Orthodox Jews take these articles of faith pretty lightly.

But do you take them lightly?

Yes I do, I think. I don't attempt to define the notion of God. For me even that isn't important.

But do you believe that the Messiah is still to come?

Well, I find it very difficult to believe in a Messiah. I think a lot of Jews do. I'm prepared to bet that he hasn't come yet from the evidence. Yet, I stand yet to be amazed when he does come.

Do you have an expectation of what might happen if he did come?

We tend to keep that very vague. I mean, you know, there is an idea that all sorts of strange things will happen which will result in a complete reshaping of the world and human values and human relationships. The point I'm making is that Judaism itself accepts that practice is really very central. That is the framework on which you base your life and by that you come, hopefully, to understand more about the mysteries of where we come from, the nature of divinity, the nature of where we're going.

And within that observance, of course, the family is the focus.

The family is a key focus, it's not the only focus. I think the key focus in Judaism, which of course is something which Christianity has certainly inherited, is the principal moral value of the sanctity of human life. But Judaism has some other wonderful aspects which are hardly ever considered. I mean, believing in democracy. It didn't like leaders. If you look at the biblical account of kings – I don't mean the chapter Kings – I mean the whole concept of kingship. It's something which is greeted with some concern about the nature of untrammelled power. The concept of an independent judiciary is very much a Jewish concept. The whole structure of Judaism, certainly since Talmudic times, has provided an entire structure for the way you live and to some extent think. Consequently faith almost takes a second line. Faith is important, but the wrong faith may be dangerous. Therefore maybe it's better to be structured, disciplined and come to think in the right sort of way.

Are there any rock-bottom beliefs without which you could not be considered to be observing your Judaism?

Monotheism is obviously one. And monotheism brings in a whole concept of fidelity. Obviously there are 613 commandments. They're all important. They don't actually have any kind of pecking order, but some of them are key to how we live. For example, respect for the Sabbath, which is something which is completely lost in modern society.

How does your family conduct the Sabbath?

We are fairly strict about that. At home we don't answer the telephone, don't turn on the television set, don't cook.

Do you turn on the light?

No, no. I must admit if I'm honest I probably do, but my children wouldn't.

What do you do?

Talk, read, interact, go for walks, occasionally study even. I generally go to synagogue in the morning on Saturday and very occasionally in the afternoon.

Jewish prayer again is part of observance. But what about private prayer?

Jewish prayer is interesting because Jewish prayer actually is also a collective thing. In Judaism there is the concept of the *minyan*, which is essentially the notion that you have 10 people who, by being together, are more significant than if you pray on your own. There's a notion that its preferable to pray within a community. Community is very important and I think that may be one of the reasons why in the past Jewish society has been so integrated. One of the issues now I think for many Jews is the relationship with the State of Israel and how a modern Jewish secular society behaves and what the true religious values are within that society. It's a very difficult issue for us I think.

Does the regime leave space for individual prayer and individual contact with God, whoever he may be?

Yes, it does. Of course one of the things about Judaism is that – and I think it's great – we do not have a defined answer to any question. There isn't one way of doing something. There isn't one way of being observant. So we don't have somebody who intercedes on our behalf. The rabbi is not a priest essentially in Judaism, not somebody who takes decisions which have been unified by the whole church. What is interesting about the Talmud is that it's basically a dispute, it's a dispute between rabbis. So the rabbis argue about what the law should be and the concept quite clearly is that there's no clear-cut defined single law. Therefore if you have a problem, a practical problem, for example, if you're trying to work out, in my field of medicine, whether or not you should go for a termination of pregnancy, one rabbi might give one decision, another rabbi might give a totally different decision. There isn't a single view. There will be guidelines, but those guidelines might vary in their interpretation.

To what extent does that lead to a sort of spiritual free-for-all?

There is the Halakhah which is the legal framework, the

skeleton on which Judaism is based. That is firmly established, so you can't transgress the basic rules and the basic commandments.

What is the Jewish concept of the soul?

There's a powerful word for it in Hebrew, and in fact very often communities are counted biblically by the number of souls in that community, even though the soul is regarded as immaterial. I think that the soul is the part of us which is divine. We are made in the image of God and perhaps that soul is part of that image as well.

You have three children growing up in the same faith. Would you be distressed if they were to marry out of your faith?

It's a question I'm often asked. First of all they are fundamentally more religious than I am, and it's rather unlikely they would marry a non-Jew. But I would be very surprised whether we would reject them or not support them over that kind of decision. That would be to me unthinkable. But clearly a continuity is important to Jews. We are a very tiny community. We are assailed on all sides. The assimilation in Britain means that now probably there are no more than a quarter of a million Jews living in Britain and many of those aren't at all observant. The notion of the 'chosen people' isn't elitist. It means that you actually have a message, the prime message being the Ten Commandments. But also that you have these basic values which include things like justice, equality and democracy, which are very firmly embedded in Judaism, and respect for life. That's why, of course, a war in the Middle East is so fundamentally a threat to our whole existence. I don't mean our physical existence, I mean our whole spiritual existence.

Nonetheless, does the concept of the 'chosen people' in today's world give you any uneasiness?

Well, it's an obligation, it's not an advantage to be chosen. Believe me, we don't see it in any way as an elitist thing.

It sets you aside though.

It only sets you aside in terms of the need to live a life that most people would find very difficult. For example, why keep the dietary laws? They don't have any sense to them, they're extremely inconvenient. Why keep the Sabbath, it's extremely inconvenient, why not ride on a bus, why not go and enjoy yourself a bit more, turn on the television.

But what are the answers?

Well the answer is that there is a framework which seems difficult to justify, but is justified because it's a way of coming to a disciplined existence. I know for myself that if I hadn't had that framework, I would have been probably totally irresponsible in my life, I would have gone completely haywire. When I think of my existence as an undergraduate, coming to terms with the fact that I ought to be Jewish again was quite an important thing.

Let's speak about the work that dominates your life and your reputation: dealing with infertility. The remark is often made that scientists these days are 'playing God'. What do you make of the phrase?

I think it's the highest thing we can do. I would say that that is absolutely admirable. We are made in the image of God, therefore we copy him. What we mustn't do is supplant God. So what we are doing is not creating life in the test tube, but using what's already available to us plus our knowledge, to enhance the protection and maintenance of human life.

When you can't verify exactly what God would require, you are thrown upon your own responsibilities. You have made decisions that have shocked people, you've allowed lesbians to have infertility treatment, and those with HIV, decisions right at the edge of social acceptability. Do you have sleepless nights about it?

It doesn't happen very often that one has sleepless nights. But I would turn the question on its head. You could argue that to refuse to treat a lesbian couple is playing God. You could argue to refuse to treat somebody who has a disease from which they might die, like HIV, is playing God. Why is it your right to withhold that treatment? I think those are important questions … they are questions of justice, they are questions of equality. What I found very interesting was that when I did treat somebody who was HIV-positive, after very careful thinking about it, there wasn't any orthodox religious authority that said anything other than that was very well thought through. All the rabbinical people who I discussed it with couldn't see a reason why that treatment shouldn't go on. They would have more difficulty with the lesbian. But I'm afraid I differ from the Orthodox Jewish church in their attitude towards sexually-active, non-heterosexual partnerships.

You spoke of referring to rabbinical advice before you make these decisions, so you do feel answerable to a body of knowledge, scholarship and interpretation at every point in your work.

Well, not only rabbinical. Colleagues too. When we finally treated an HIV-positive woman, it was after I had discussed it with members of the Human Fertilisation and Embryology Authority, the regulatory body, it was after I had discussed it with senior colleagues at the Hammersmith Hospital. The initial reaction from my own team was very hostile. Within some months the great majority of my team were very clear that we should be offering this treatment to that particular couple.

And cloning ... does that present problems?

Well, I'm now going to give a hostage to fortune. I don't understand fundamentally why there's anything wrong with cloning. The truth is that there are 25,000 clones, human clones, walking around in Britain at the moment, and they are much more similar than any man-made clone. They are identical twins, and when you start thinking about that, you then have to ask yourself what is the objection. Well, the objection is certainly there in terms of our general morality. In fact, Judaism doesn't have a strong view. Judaism probably would not see anything wrong with cloning. It wouldn't see any obvious clear-cut reason why cloning should be prohibited except on two grounds: one would be a religious interdiction, which would be that if you were doing something which might make a child unhealthy, abnormal or likely to die, that would be unacceptable. Religious law would not approve of that under any circumstances. I think rightly. That would be my moral position too. So that's one argument against cloning. The other argument is not nearly so clear-cut in Jewish law, but it's much more clear-cut in civil law. It's the notion that you're treating a child as a commodity. You're trying to impose on a child an expectation of something that you want from it, which isn't naturally given. What Jewish rabbis will say very jokingly – and they have said this in my presence – is that all Jewish parents expect things of their children. But this is fundamentally different and I think there's a problem. That's why I would not approve of taking tissue or blood cells from a child yet to be born to try and help its older brother. It seems to me that to create a child specifically to treat another child imposes

152

on that younger child huge burdens, which it may not actually want to shoulder when it grows.

Dealing as you do with embryos and helping to create new life, in Judaism at what point in the growth of an embryo does it become human?

There isn't a defined moment in Judaism. A child actually achieves human rights when it's born, at the moment of birth. Before that it's not the same as a born human. There is a notion in Judaism that there's a gradual increase to the respect accorded to a developing child as it develops.

Does that understanding govern the point at which you intervene?

In Judaism we are allowed to terminate pregnancy at any stage if a mother's life is threatened by the pregnancy. That's definitely clearly asserted. Abortion is legal, but of course it has to be justified on the grounds that you are saving life, but that would include saving health because health is part of life.

To the other end of life, what is the Jewish perspective on euthanasia?

Very difficult. The Jewish notion of euthanasia most people would regard as being pretty strict. We do not take life, adult human life. Euthanasia is quite clearly forbidden. If somebody is moribund, and there are definitions of that word in Hebrew which are important, then there are certain things that you are allowed not to do. For example, you may withhold certain treatments which might keep somebody alive and in pain, but you would still be expected to give food and fluids in nearly all cases. Turning off a life support system is quite complex in Judaism and there are many arguments. Again, there's not a single view, but the general trend is to be fairly restrictive.

Do Jews believe in life after death?

Umm, we do … we believe in the world to come, but it's a very loose concept and it doesn't really mean very much.

What are your own personal expectations?

To tell you the truth, I don't have much expectation about tomorrow, let alone worry about these concepts. I find it very difficult to believe in useful things going on for me after death.

Yet the Christian faith focusses on the Resurrection and Christ coming to defeat death.

Yes, Christians have much stronger views of things like heaven and hell than we do too. We don't really believe in paradise, and hell to us is an interesting connotation, but it's not the same connotation as it is in the Christian faith. Christ really promulgated what are essentially Jewish values. Loving your neighbour as yourself is very much a Jewish concept. It comes very much from the Five Books of Moses. Where we take issue is the notion of his divinity, because we would argue that we're all the sons of God, or the daughters of God. We would regard ourselves as being equal, and we would not be prepared to regard him as being a Messiah. What Jesus certainly did was to establish a very effective and important Western religion, for which we have increasing regard.

❖

13

ZIAUDDIN SARDAR

'The beginning of knowledge'

Ziauddin Sardar was born in Pakistan and brought up in Hackney, London, by his Muslim parents. He is a writer and lecturer whose fascination with the history and philosophy of his faith has taken him around the world in search of a form of Islam that will take Islam into a more consensual, reasoned future. He has charted his search in some 40 books, and early in 2004 published his autobiography, Desperately Seeking Paradise.

Most Muslims learn their Koran from their mothers, and if the mothers are not original Arabic-speaking, they don't take what they are teaching for granted. They themselves are learning in the process. So what my mother was doing by trying to answer my questions, was also trying to learn herself. It was a mutual learning process. She would read the words of the Koran in Arabic, and I would be asked to repeat it, so that I can memorise some of it, which most Muslims do. Then I would ask 'What does it mean?' She would then look into commentaries and tell me what the particular words meant. And so we engaged in a dialogue, that went on continuously.

How is the Koran different from the Bible?

Well it is a radically different book. Many people describe it as a epic poem, but it's more like a symphony where each note has a specific place. And it's not a very big book like the Bible. It's a comparatively short book. That's why it is easy to memorise. It has a rhythm and rhyme, and it's a book that argues with itself. Essentially, the Koran is a book of guidance, guidance for humanity. But it is interesting to note that almost one-third of the Koran is devoted to extolling the virtues of reason, of thinking, of studying nature, of seeking knowledge, self-reflection, inner reflection.

Is the Koran the final book, the end of all knowledge?

No. The Koran is not the end of all knowledge, the Koran is the beginning of all knowledge. Most Muslims accept that the Koran is the Word of God. That is a definition of a Muslim. If you do not accept that the Koran is the Word of God, then you are not a Muslim. That's where it begins. It provides an ethical and moral perspective on life, on the universe, on everything, including of course knowledge … it's the beginning of knowledge, it's not the end of knowledge.

Is it capable of many interpretations?

Absolutely. You can only have an interpreted relationship with the text. If you think the text is eternal then that interpretative relationship goes on and on. It's a text full of metaphors, parables, and all varieties of complex interpretation.

Does it live in your life daily? Do you find yourself returning to it and perhaps finding new insights?

Absolutely. Most Muslims do that regularly. The problem is that Muslims nowadays do that almost on autopilot.

But what about you?

I think because I'm a writer I try to look at the verses in a totally different way each time. Of course I look at them in translation. My Arabic is not very good, and it is commonly said that the language of the Koran is Arabic. But actually the language of the Koran is the language of the Koran – there are a finite number of words that are used in the Koran and I struggle with these words through translation and come across new meanings and new insights.

It was your mother who taught you what the concept of 'paradise' was in the Koran. Can you explain it to me?

Most people think that paradise is a fixed place of gardens, rivers, of milk and honey and beautiful women. … Part of this is Muslim folklore, part of it is orientalist interpretation. The Muslim paradise is very sophisticated. I think it is important to appreciate that the Islamic concept of God is very different from the Christian or Jewish concept of God, and therefore our notion of paradise is also radically different. Essentially, in Islam, God is beyond description. He cannot be imagined by the human mind at all. Nothing we can do, can actually give us even an inkling of what the entity of God is like. So the only way we can understand God is through his attributes. And in Islam there are 99 attributes. Such as: He is the beautiful, He is the beginning, He is the first and He is the last, He is the merciful, He is the beneficent, and so on. So it is only through His attributes that we can actually appreciate God. And similarly with paradise – only through attributes we can really appreciate what paradise is. So paradise is all about metaphor, it's all about parable. When we talk of paradise as full of milk and honey, it's an ontological argument. What do we associate with honey: sweetness, health. We associate gardens with peace.

Does the concept of paradise affect the prospect of dying?

Well, Muslims very strongly believe in accountability. They strongly believe there's a life after death. So we have a different notion of time. For us time does not end with death. Time is a continuous tapestry in which our present life is a part of a much greater notion of time. And so the time after death is much bigger than time in this life. Therefore we are constantly preparing for life after death. We're constantly aware that we are going to be accountable for everything we do in this life. This is why I think it is not unusual to find Muslims who are not too concerned about death.

You are from the Sunni tradition. Do you feel very separate from the Shia tradition? Is it a very alien thing to you?

The answer is yes and no. There are certain things in the Shia tradition that I would not subscribe to at all. For example, they have this notion the Imams are descendants of the Prophet. And they are supposed to be *'masoom'* meaning 'innocent'.

I cannot believe that a man can be totally and utterly above sin. It's a very fundamental difference. However, Shias are very much part of the Islamic community. I do not feel separate from them at all. In fact I have many Shia friends, and it was only after the Iranian Revolution that I learned that they were Shia.

What role does the Prophet have in your belief?

The Prophet is the receiver of Revelation. The Koran was revealed over a 23-year period, and basically the Koran is commenting on the actions, the daily activities, and the struggles that the Prophet is engaged in. Therefore the Koran has a context. You cannot just take any verse as some Muslims are prone to do and interpret in any way whatsoever. The life of the Prophet and the Koran go together, and the life of the Prophet is the model for us to follow. For me the life of the Prophet is very important. I try to imbibe some of his attributes and characteristics. Now most Muslims want to model themselves almost exactly on him. He had a beard – so they want to have a beard. But you may have noticed that I do not have a beard. I do not regard the physical characteristics of the Prophet as something that we have to emulate. Neither do I regard certain other aspects of the Prophet which are very contextual to the period that he actually lived in. But there are certain characteristics of the Prophet which I think are universal. For example his sense of generosity, which was absolute, very deep. His notion of forgiveness. He was persecuted for decades, his followers were tortured, he was driven out of Mecca. When he returns to Mecca he says 'This day there'll be no retribution – you are all forgiven.' That is an incredible notion of generosity and forgiveness which I think is essential for Muslims to imbibe.

Your book – Desperately Seeking Paradise – *is about a search, and you tell how in 1972 two men knocked on your door. You were then a young man in your teens. And they were the Talibi Jamat, a particular wing of Islam, and off you went with them.*

As a young man I was quite active in the Muslim student community. So I knew a little bit about Muslim communities and various Muslim groups, but I hadn't made up my mind which particular group to belong to. So I was quite open at that period. So at the moment the Talibi Jamat people came I did not want to go with them. But my mother was very keen to push me out. She thought she had taught me enough. It was time for me to learn Islam from other people and she knew that there are different interpretations of Islam.

What did they teach you that endures?

I think they taught me the quest for paradise is a worthy quest. It's not just a quest for something that is utopian, something that is beyond life. It's also a quest that is very real and is part of this life as well, in the sense that we need to create a paradise on this earth.

So that's quite political.

That's very political and I think most Muslims tend to be very political. The important thing about Islam is that it has a very strong sense of justice. If you go back to the Koran, it repeatedly asks the believers to do justice. And by justice it means social justice, and distributive justice. You need to treat people with equality, with respect, with dignity. Their rights have to be respected. So I have a very strong notion of justice, which makes me political, and I think that's what makes most Muslims political.

It makes you left-wing, but it doesn't make most Muslims left-wing, does it?

Of course it makes some Muslims right-wing too. Aspects of Islam can be interpreted in a number of different ways. The people who are approaching and studying Islam who are trying to gain guidance from the Koran are human and the Muslim community is a human community. So we have left-wing and right-wing, we have secularists, we have multi-culturalists, we have Evangelical, we have revolutionaries.

And in your own life, you also explored Sufism.

Sufism is, as far as I'm concerned, an integral part of Islam. The Prophet himself used to meditate. Now different Sufi *tariqas* as they are called – groups – will have different ways of doing 'zikr', or remembrance of Allah. I joined a particular group which basically consisted of white, middle-class English converts. Some of them came from California, some of them came from Hampstead. And essentially what they were looking for was a new high. In my opinion they were genuine Sufis and they did take me into a trip. Their way of doing 'zikr' was actually to form a circle every night and to recite 'Allah Hu!' which is just to recite the names of God and dance. Now it did get me high, but I did think that there were some serious problems. What concerns me about mysticism – and it's not just Sufism, I think all kinds of mysticism – is this idea of relationship between the disciple and the master. I just am not willing to enter in any relationship where I cannot question. And I think that is the basic view of the Koran. If you look at the Koran, the Koran is full of questions from beginning to end and it insisted that believers ask questions. The Koran is not about blind faith. It insists that the believers keep asking questions continuously, because even if they have asked a question and received the answer, the answer may actually change, so they have to ask that question again.

You spent a lot of time in Saudi Arabia. And the form of Islam there is Wahabism. What was your experience of Wahabism?

When you actually arrive in Jedda, what you notice is that everybody is wearing white, right? It's very, very hot. The walls are whitewashed, the people are wearing white, white toupes. Everywhere there's white. There is no shade of grey of any kind. The only other colour you saw was that women had to wear black veils by law. Now the moment this hits you, you know there's something very peculiar about this society. First of all there are no shades of grey in terms of colour, and then the only colour is an unjust imposition on women. Black is the worst thing to actually wear in that kind of climate, because black absorbs all the heat, it traps all the heat. So you have men wandering about wearing white with loose clothing so air is circulating. They are nice and cool – and the women are basically trapped, women exist in a heat trap. Immediately you see there's some notion of injustice that is deeply ingrained in this society.

Is that part of their faith, though?

That's more or less become part of their faith, that women have to be covered up and not just covered up, but have to cover up in black, by law.

It raises the whole relationship of Islam and its attitude to women…

All the ideas of relationship between men and women are essentially based on a single verse of the Koran, which is a very famous verse, known as the 'modesty verse'. The Koran asked the believers – believing men and believing women – to lower their gaze and guard their modesty. Now the way this has been interpreted, as many feminist Muslim scholars have pointed out, is that modesty only applies to women. And the idea that women should lower their gaze and guard their modesty has been transformed into the idea that they should be covered, in a veil, and locked up inside the house.

What's your view of this in your own life?

My wife doesn't cover her hair, my daughter doesn't wear a veil either. Both of them work. There are certain Muslims who will argue that this is not the best way for Muslim women to be. But there are other interpretations as well, a huge number of interpretations.

What disenchanted you about Wahabism?

What disenchanted me was the notion of time. You asked earlier does knowledge end with the Koran, and I said 'No, knowledge begins with the Koran.' Now as far as the Wahabis are concerned knowledge ends with the Koran and also morality ends in eighth-century Arabia. So they have adopted all the contextual things in the life of the Prophet. There's no notion of time, that in fact morality can evolve with time. There's no notion of multiple interpretation – there's only one Puritan-like faith, and only one notion of truth.

And this is the faith that Osama Bin Laden follows?

Not just Osama Bin Laden, but many people who basically claim to be fighting for Islam and are engaging in terrorism – most of them tend to be Wahabis.

You continue your pursuit of the ideal Islamic state and in 1979 you rejoiced in the Iranian Revolution because you say it 'crystallised the zeitgeist'.

Well, this takes me back to my strong feeling for justice. I thought the Iranian Revolution will actually be a socialist revolution – will distribute wealth, will provide equal opportunity for men and women, and most important, it will be a knowledge-based revolution in that there will be mass education available to all, there'll be progress in science and technology and research and so on.

What did you find when you got there?

I found it was totally the opposite! Most of my idealistic notions of revolution were stopped in their tracks. Now what am I seeking constantly? I am seeking an interpretation of Islam that is at once relevant and contemporary and true to the teachings of Islam. And that to me is ultimately paradise. It is not a fixed paradise – it's a paradise that we constantly struggle to shape. Because what we are trying to understand is how to implement the notion of justice, the notion of beauty, the notion of thought and learning, the notion of dissent that we learn from Islamic ethics, and that requires constant struggle.

Let's stay with the Iranian Revolution for the time being, because that instituted the shariah – the shariah which is the codified law of Islam – as the law of the state. Now this is a crucial development in the modern world, that there are now increasingly Islamic countries who follow the Sharia. What problem does that present for you?

Well, the idea of the shariah is frozen in history. Shariah is not just Islamic law – it is also ethics and morality. Now if you freeze law in history, then you have also frozen your ethics and morality in history. And it was also dehumanised. Most Muslims believe that the shariah is divine. But in fact a great deal of the shariah – I would say something like 95 per cent of it – is socially constructed in history. In other words, we had these believers who were struggling to implement their own notions of paradise. And for them it was a dynamic exercise, and for us it has become a very ossified and a fixed and a static exercise. And that's why I think it's so problematic.

Can the Sharia be updated?

It's not a question of shariah being updated, it's a question of shariah being re-interpreted, for us to come up with new ideas of what the relevance of Islam is in contemporary life and hence shape a law that is more up to date and more contemporary.

In your search, you've come to admire the form of Islam practised in Malaysia...

South-east Asian Islam, it seems to me, is much more open, much more liberal. The idea of plurality is central to it, so you have multiple interpretations. But even there the Wahabi influence is very strong. There is a struggle going on between open multi-interpretative Islam and a fixed notion of Islam.

And where within that picture does the tolerance of non-Islamic religions come?

Well in a sense, Islam is very ecumenical. First of all, Islam recognises that it doesn't have a monopoly of truth. Truth has been revealed to other faiths as well. Specifically Jews and Christians are people of the book, the Bible. And if you look at the life of the Prophet the respect and reverence he has shown to Judaism and Christianity is clearly evident. It's not just Christians and Jews, but Muslims believe that every nation, every community has had a Prophet and has some notion of truth.

You came up against a variety of intolerances when Salman Rushdie published The Satanic Verses. *You yourself were appalled by the book, but then you were appalled by the Muslim reaction to it.*

Well I read *The Satanic Verses* on a flight from Kuala Lumpur to London. A 13-, 14-hour flight. So I started reading it, quite innocently and as I carried on reading, I started shaking and then eventually when I got to the sacrilegious bits I became quite frozen. It had an absolutely stunning impact on me. I felt as though I was raped. My inner sanctum was violated. Everything I hold dear was systematically abused, and described in an horrific way. Take the scenes where he's talking about the Prophet's wives. Now he gives them exactly the same physical descriptions, the same physical attributes, the names are the same – almost everything's the same as in the Koran. But of course they are prostitutes and they're described in derogatory terms. It is impossible for a believing Muslim not to be affected by it.

Did you feel he had the right to write it?

That is a very interesting question. I'm willing to forgive him for actually writing it. I'm strongly in favour of writing as an exercise and reading. I mean the first word that was revealed to the Prophet is 'read'. So reading and writing are very important for Muslims as a whole. And in Islamic history, books are fought with books. In fact my response was that it is a book that has attacked us, and we therefore must attack it back with a book. Which is in fact what I tried to do.

But you didn't want to see it burned?

No, no.

Or the fatwa?

Most certainly I did not want the fatwa. I think after Rushdie I was the second person to be most upset by the fatwa. Because what the fatwa did was tell me as a Muslim intellectual that I was not capable of defending the Islamic position. Indeed I was not even capable of performing my social right of standing up on behalf of the Muslims and saying 'No, we can fight this book with another book.' So I felt that made me redundant. I was very upset by the fatwa.

And did you feel that the whole incident crystallised something about the ongoing tensions between Islam and other societies?

Yes. Absolutely, absolutely. What we are getting are two

different kinds of extremes. It's become very much a battle of extremes. On one side we have this liberal secularist form of fundamentalism and extremism which can only paint religion in general and Muslims in particular with the colours of evil.

Where do we find that?

Where do we find that? If you look at the case of a Dutch film maker, Theo van Gogh, who made the film *Submission*. The film is saying that all Muslim women are systematically abused and degraded by their husbands, by their uncles, by their fathers and Islam is evil. And this is how Islam treats women. It's a very extremist representation of Islam and therefore it generated an extremist response. He got a knife. My reaction is 'A plague on both your houses.' I want to move away from extremism of all kinds. And to do that one needs a cultured liberalist space where these things can be discussed openly. Nobody will say that the plight of the Muslim women does not need attention, or that Islamic law regarding women needs to be reformed. There is no question about it. But it has to be done within the parameters of Islam.

Is it possible to evolve an enlightened, reformed form of Islam?

Oh very much, very much. I see many signs which are already happening. For example the personal aspect of Islamic law has been totally transformed in Morocco. There's a new law that came on the statute book in February 2004, and in my opinion, it's probably every bit as advanced as some of the things we have in Britain.

Are your own ideas evolving?

My ideas are constantly evolving. I think as a believer, you can't be static. I must confess openly that I am constantly on the boundaries of doubt. I think when believers say that their faith is so strong that they cannot doubt, then there's something wrong. My understanding of Islam is certainly transformed in the last 30 years and, each step in the journey, I've learned something new. In fact I'm changing all the time.

14

PHILIP PULLMAN

'Moral codes are a very interesting example of how religions get things wrong'

Philip Pullman is now one of the world's most celebrated authors of books for children, but read by adults too. He was for some 18 years a teacher – for 12 years of children, then for six years of trainee teachers. In the course of that time he began publishing: first in 1982 Count Karlstein, *then in 1986* The Ruby in the Smoke, *the first of a quartet of books about a young Victorian girl, Sally Lockhart. Some 20 books have followed.*

His most outstanding success has undoubtedly been the trilogy of books His Dark Materials *which have sold in their millions, been made into a play for Britain's National Theatre, and a film with a screenplay by Tom Stoppard. The three,* Northern Lights *(The Golden Compass in the USA),* The Subtle Knife *and* The Amber Spyglass *have won many awards, including The Carnegie Medal, The Guardian Children's Book Award, and for* The Amber Spyglass, *The Whitbread Book of the Year Award.*

The trilogy encompasses a vast narrative of epic scale in which a child, Lyra, moves through parallel universes, finds friends and allies, is pursued by fantastical creatures in her battle against the Magisterium, for the destiny of the world. Such is the grandeur of the concept and the multiplicity of references that I was keen to know how he had begun.

✢

I began by stealing an atmosphere from the second book of *Paradise Lost*, by that I mean that the descriptions in Books one and two of *Paradise Lost* are a landscape of hell – the fallen angels having just been hurled out of heaven, defeated by the forces of heaven, regrouping themselves and plotting to over-throw the powers in a more subtle way. That was something I first encountered when I was 17, doing A levels at school and it made such an impression on me at the time – not so much at that stage for the profundity of the idea so much as the power of the language – I physically felt my hair standing on end, my skin bristling, my heart racing, as we read through this won-derful stuff. And that is something that always remained with me; little phrases, passages of rhythm, little talismans of this wonderful piece, remained with me for a very long time. And eventually, the idea came to me that I'd like to do a book using this sort of landscape. Previously, I'd done stuff which was entirely realistic. I tried to stick to the real world. Here I had a sort of licence to go and be fantastical.

You've also paid tribute to your debt to Blake.

Well, Blake was a great Miltonian of course. And I think the truest thing anyone's ever said about Milton is, the reason Milton wrote in fetters when he wrote of angels and heaven, and at liberty when he wrote of devils and hell, is that he was a true poet and of the Devil's party without knowing it.

This question about being of the Devil's party is quite problematic. Let me just read from The Amber Spyglass *in an attempt to pin you down. It's an angel, Balthamos, speaking: 'Balthamos said quietly: "The Authority, God, the Creator, the Lord, Yahweh, El, the King, the Father, the Almighty – those were all names he gave himself. He was never the Creator. He was an angel like ourselves; the first angel too, the most powerful. But he was formed of dust as we are, and dust is only a name for what happens when matter begins to understand itself."' Do you believe in God?*

No, I don't believe in anything, any being that could be encompassed by the term, God. I sort of believe what Balthamos was saying there. Only 'sort of' because of course, he's a character in a story and he's not the narrator of the story; and even the narrator of the story is not me. I am several layers of distance behind that. But nevertheless, what Balthamos is voicing there is something that comes from what I call the myth. Now, as I was writing this novel, I was simultaneously writing something else. I was simultaneously writing a sort of creation myth that would lie behind it all, which is no way explicit in the book except in those words of Balthamos.

The notion is that matter comes into being by itself, spontaneously, out of nothing. There's no need for a creator. A creator is entirely mysterious, irrelevant. But the first of the angels is the one who later becomes known by all these names, and in the book, he's referred to as the Authority. And by the time we reach the end of the book, the Authority's very old, decrepit, senile and longing for nothing more than death and dissolution. And this actually is something you can read in the Bible. If we read the Bible from beginning to end, we see the first appearance of God is rather sprightly and mischievous and young. And furthermore, he is able to engage in, not only in conversation with human beings, but he actually walks up and down the garden with them. Later on, he withdraws. He refuses to let Abraham look at him, for example. So, he's changing. And later on in the Book of Daniel, he's referred to as the Ancient of Days – well, he's getting older, isn't he? He's clearly getting older. He's not an unchangeable presence.

You say God's getting older, so is he going to die?

In my story, he does, yes. But what I'm intending to show by that is that the old idea of God as being a person who's up there, who loves us and looks after us and controls us and watches the fall of every sparrow, that idea has had its time. It's dead.

So, this is an account of where our beliefs come from?

No. I wouldn't put it like that. It might turn out to be an account of where my beliefs have come from, but first and foremost, it's a story. I didn't set out to write this thing in order to embody a myth. The myth was something for my own private needs. I needed to have some sort of solid ground on which the rest could be erected. But the most important thing as far as the reader is concerned is the story of what happens: event succeeding event, explanations of things that were mysterious gradually becoming apparent. Consequences being worked out. That's how stories work, and I'm concerned with a story rather than anything else.

Do you see the world's religions and all their ramifications as stories, that it is the nature of consciousness to explain itself in stories?

Yes, that's a very interesting line, which could lead us into neurological science and all sorts of things. But it's certainly obvious that all religions have explained themselves to their own adherents, and to those whom they wish to convert in terms of stories: there was a man who ...; and then this happened; and then he died; and then he rose again – that's a story.

And do you believe that myths, Greek myths, Roman myths, all the legends of different groups and people, are their attempt to search out explanations for why we're here and what the world is about?

172

Yes, we explain everything in terms of stories. The other day, I was in my bedroom at the time, and I heard a great big bang outside. And I looked out of the window and somebody had crashed their car into my garden wall, and was sitting in the car. We called the ambulance, and everything else. But how did this happen? The neighbours were all worried how it happened. Eventually, we worked out what the story was. How it happened that she had done this and crashed the car, and then we were satisfied. Until then, we were puzzled but once we worked out how it came about, we were satisfied. This hunger for working out how things come about, is tremendously deep. It's almost insatiable, because once we've heard how this came about, we want to know how the next thing came about.

But it's full of paradox, isn't it? Because of course, every witness to an event tells a different story.

Well, it helps to remember where you're seeing things from. In the words of my favourite quotation about storytelling, the basic question is where do you put the camera? Where do you put the camera; where are you seeing it from? Now, it's possible to describe my own beliefs for example, as being both atheist and agnostic, depending on where I put the camera. If I look at the total amount of things I know, and compare it with the things I don't know, the things I know constitute the tiniest possible, remote, little speck of light in the middle of a great, vast encircling darkness; which is everything I don't know. And in all the things I don't know, there may be a God. There may be a God out there, but I don't know. However, when you move the camera, when you come in a bit and get closer to this little speck of light, it gets bigger and bigger, and finally spreads

173

out beyond the edges of the vision and fills everything you can see. Here, I can see no evidence whatever for God. So on this level, I'm an atheist; further out, I'm an agnostic; depends on where you're standing.

Well let's go into your own story then. Your grandfather was a vicar in the Church of England.

Yes, rector of a little country parish near Norwich. And I spent quite a lot of my time in his household because my father, who was in the RAF, died when I was seven, and my mother was living alone in London, working actually at the BBC. My brother and I were sort of passed along to Norfolk, which we were very happy about. We loved grandpa. We loved granny. We loved the life in the rectory. And his religion was very much a product of his time. I remember John Robinson's book, *Honest to God*, came out when he was still alive and he dismissed it with regret and scorn. That wasn't what they were about at all.

His faith, I think, had been formed in World War I, when he was an officer. And he saw the good work done by the padres of the time. It was a simple, practical one. It made people feel better. It cheered them up when they were dying.

You went to Sunday school. You sang the hymns. You knew the liturgy. When did you begin to cast a rather more critical eye?

I think when most of us do, in my teen years. I was reading all sorts of things, reading widely. The big thing then was Colin Wilson's *The Outsider*, a wonderful book for teenagers to read because it leads you on to all sorts of other things. So reading and thinking more and more about things, and also reading the poets.

174

So, what did you then make of the iconography and the dogma; the doctrine of the Church?

It seemed nonsense. It seemed incredible.

So, it's a question of faith.

Yes, but it's not easy to believe something if you know it to be nonsense. I know one of the famous theologians – Tertullian, I think – said, 'It is certain because it is impossible.' Well, I haven't yet reached the point when this makes sense to me.

Do you remember what the epicycles were? When we had the Ptolemaic system of astronomy, everything went around the earth, and the planets and the sun, they all revolved around the earth. The trouble was this didn't match up with observation because sometimes the planets would go faster, and sometimes they'd go slower, and sometimes they might even appear to go backwards for a day or two. How could this happen if they were all going smoothly around the earth? And they came up with this idea of epicycles. They're actually not going around in a simple circle but in a lot of little circles all around one big circle, and then it makes sense – 'Ha, got it now; epicycles.' But time went on, and more observations were made and still these things didn't seem to fit. So then, they had epicycles on epicycles. The whole thing was getting more and more complicated and more paradoxical, more and more difficult until the great discovery was made. The realisation. Now, supposing we see it another way; supposing the earth goes round the sun, all the difficulties vanish. Now, I believe, these epicycles are very like all the paradoxes that clever Christians in the present age are forced to come up with. Such as the one, I think it's from Simeon Weil, 'this great presence, which is like an absence'. I mean, that's nonsense. It's an epicycle. It's an attempt to let logic deal with something which logic can't deal with.

175

But haven't you just offered up a hostage there though, because if there is an arena of human experience which logic can't deal with, you have to concede that it must exist beyond logic?

Yes. Of course it does. Logic is very good in its place, but it doesn't cover everything. No, I don't regulate my daily life by means of logic. I regulate it by habit, by superstition, by guesswork, by all sorts of things.

By moral code?

Well, moral codes are a very interesting example of how religion, I think, gets it wrong, and how I wish religious people would be a bit more modest. According to religious people, all morality comes from the fount of goodness which is God, and all moral teachings are religious in origin.

Well, no, they're not. A lot of moral teachings come from literature. A lot of moral teachings come from simple observation. This is where moral teaching comes from. We don't need a supernatural explanation.

Did you, nonetheless, take on the tenets of Christian morality, as you grew up?

In some respects, yes. And I think I probably break the ones that everybody else breaks. But I think the ones that make sense in a general human context are the ones that involve harm to other people. Thou shalt not murder. Thou shalt not steal. Thou shalt not bear false witness. Those make sense, but then, they make sense without a supernatural origin.

But given the decline in religious faith and in concepts set out in The Sermon on the Mount, if coming generations abandon them completely, will people still feel the idea that underpins, say, the Ten Commandments is a good one, or not?

I don't think the morality embodied in the commandments doesn't make sense, or will ever fade away, because this is a sensible way of regulating human society. It's a sensible way which has evolved by natural selection over the course of millennia. This is a good way to behave to other people.

When you lost your own faith, did you have a sense of loss?

I had a sense of liberation. I suddenly saw that all sorts of things were possible. I don't mean it was possible to do naughty things it was forbidden to before. What I meant was, it's possible to see and believe certain things. It's possible to unbelieve certain things. I never felt the need for the psychological support or crutch which I know some people feel. I never did.

Let's go into some of the actual nature of His Dark Materials. *The use of vocabulary, 'the Magisterium', 'the Board of Oblation' – oblation isn't a word you run across very often. It's in the liturgy of course. 'The society of the work of the Holy Spirit.' I mean, these are all taken from the Christian Church.*

Well, they're made-up titles, but they're made up from a kit of parts which the Catholic Church has kindly prepared for us. That's what they're intended to mean.

So, are you gunning for the Catholic Church?

I'm happy to have it in place as a villain. But we're talking about another world, remember, and we're talking about a world in which the Catholic Church develops in a very different way, because Calvin became the Pope in the history of Lyra's world, and instead of having one single figure and one single body of authority, the Church in Lyra's world is actually split into a number of little constituent and warring and rival colleges and bodies of authority. So, they're all fighting amongst themselves.

But where do you feel this great antagonism? Is it a seething resentment of the damage that you believe churches and established religions do?

It's a deep anger – and yes, horror – at the excesses of cruelty and infamy that have been carried out in the name of a supernatural power. And it's not only the Catholic Church that is guilty of this. The Protestants were just as guilty of burning the Catholics and their towns, and of hanging the witches. And both sides are guilty of persecuting the Jews. And then you get Muslims killing Hindus, and Hindus killing Muslims, and Sikhs killing Muslims and Hindus. The list goes on and on. I think it was a physicist, Steve Weinberg, who said the truest thing about this. He said, good people have done good things, and bad people have done bad things without the help of religion, but for good people to do evil things, that takes religion.

So, where does this anger have its root? Because anger is quite a disturbing component of a personality, isn't it?

I don't think I'm an angry person. But there's righteous anger, isn't there? Which is kind of prophetic. And I'd like to think that the anger I feel at the excesses and cruelties of religion is righteous anger. You see parents in a suburb in the United Kingdom, spitting and throwing stones and hurling abuse at little children on the way to school, because they belong, not even to a different religion but merely to a different sect. This is Christians shouting and spitting at Christians. Religion is to blame for that.

178

There is another account, of course, which is the abundance of charity, the selflessness, good deeds, sacrifice, that Christianity and other religions harness and focus on the needy of the world, the consolations of prayer and introspection, the beauty of liturgy, music, cathedrals. There's a huge range of richness that the Church brings to humanity.

That's perfectly true and as far as the aesthetic component of it goes – the beauty of the liturgy, the hymns, the psalms, the Bible and so on – this is something that's very deeply part of me. Every Sunday in my childhood, I went to church. This was the time when we had the 1662 Book of Common Prayer, and the King James Bible and *Hymns Ancient and Modern – words that were well put together. So, these are very much part of the me that exists.*

Now, let's go back to His Dark Materials. *What are you suggesting as the way in which we should live, if you don't want us to be ruled by an authoritative religion?*

This is summed up in the phrase that ends the book – 'the republic of heaven'. If the Authority is no more – if the King is dead – what happens to the Kingdom of Heaven? The idea of heaven remains I think very important. It stands for a sense of community. It stands for joy. It stands for a sense that the universe and we together, have a common meaning and a common destiny, and a purpose. It stands for connectedness between these things. All these things are so important, so fundamental to what keeps me alive that I don't want to be without them. I don't want to do without heaven, but I can no longer believe in a Kingdom of Heaven. So there must be a republic of heaven of which we are free and equal citizens – and it's our duty to promote and preserve it.

So, we are citizens here and now.

Here and now, because there ain't no elsewhere.

And there's no life after death? What's going to happen to us?

This is one of the difficult moments of giving up believing. It's probably the last thing that goes when your Christian belief leaves you. Your belief in some sort of afterlife is very precious and very difficult to relinquish. But in the course of *The Amber Spyglass*, I think I've told a story about death and what happens afterwards, which satisfies me both emotionally and aesthetically and intellectually. What happens when we die is that we are sort of recycled. I mean, our bodies are clearly recycled and the different little bits, atoms, constituent parts, motes of dust that make up our consciousness, are also recycled. Nothing's lost.

In your books each individual goes through life with a daemon perched on their shoulder. Is this a soul?

It's an aspect of our personality, which in Lyra's world has become visible. Now, in my myth the daemon is conceived of as being the gift of the rebel angels. In the course of the myth, the rebel angels are on the side of right and decency and goodness and consciousness, and they're led by a figure called the Sophia – wisdom – who's a figure which I've borrowed from Gnostic myth. The rebel angels led by Sophia gave to the beings in each world a gift that would help them understand themselves and become wise. In some worlds, they gave them a daemon. In other worlds, they gave them a song that could pull down wisdom from the stars. What it does, this gift, is to help one achieve wisdom. Wisdom, which is the sort of natural status of life and consciousness, towards which we move almost gravitationally.

Do you feel as a teller of stories on such a scale, and with such a constituency of young readers, the responsibility of the story-teller?

There are many responsibilities the story-teller has. To the audience, certainly. And when you have a young audience, or an audience which includes young people, I think you have a duty to remember the wisest thing that Dr Johnson said, which is, the only end to writing is to enable the reader better to endure life, or better to enjoy it. Children need these forms of consolation just as much as adult readers do, and that's one of the responsibilities of the story-teller.

A story-teller also has a responsibility towards language. And when it comes to difficult words and complex figures of speech and so on, your responsibility there is not to avoid them. Not to think, 'Ah, that's a jolly good idea; too clever for this story though, I'll use it somewhere else.' No. You put it in. The young reader will follow it if the story's strong enough.

But the greatest responsibility of the story-teller is to the story. Towards the story, you are in a position of servant to master or mistress. And the job of the servant is to perform a job conscientiously, to turn up for work on time, to be sober in working hours, to do all the work that's necessary to prepare the way; and also, to give up common sense when the master – or the story – demands it.

'Look at the windmills.'

'Those are giants. I'm going to kill the giants for you.'

'No, master, don't be silly; they're not giants, they're windmills.'

'Ah, nonsense. They're giants I tell you. But, don't worry, I'll deal with them.'

'All right, master, as you say, giants they are.'

The story is the boss, so the story-teller has to serve the story, no matter how crazy it is.

Do you feel a responsibility to help people through your story-telling, to live out their lives without giving up?

Yes, certainly. And one of the things I was trying to do in the story, though not in an educational way, but simply because that's the way I do things, is to show my characters revelling in the beauty of the world; and seeing, as if with new eyes, how extraordinarily precious and wonderful the physical world is.

❖

15

MINETTE WALTERS

'More comfortable to be an atheist'

Minette Walters' star as a crime writer rose dramatically throughout the 1990s. Her first three novels, The Ice House, The Sculptress *and* The Scold's Bridle, *won top awards in both the UK and America and she went on to win further awards with* The Shape of Snakes *and* Fox Evil. *Writing virtually a novel a year, her most recent,* Disordered Minds, *was published in 2004. She is a prison visitor and patron of Victim Support in Dorset.*

I remember a schoolboy asking me whether I worried that I was giving people ideas on how to kill other people. And I have to say I don't worry about it, largely because there are far worse things reported in the newspapers every day – actual killings. I always feel my responsibility is to write a good story because I think that's what I'm being paid to do. That's my primary responsibility and within that responsibility I can explore ideas that matter to me. I think crusades in fiction don't work very well because a crusade can get in the way of a story. Nonetheless I hope that some of the ideas that I've put down will provoke readers to go on thinking after they've finished the book. Then I'd be happy.

You see yourself giving them a moral directive, do you?
    Yes, to a certain extent. I wouldn't like to put it in quite such

stark terms because first and foremost it's a story. But, yes, I can put some moral dilemmas before them which they explore with me and either come to a conclusion with me or not as the case may be. Then I think I'm doing a good thing.

Examine yourself as a character. What motivation would you perceive in yourself?

It's quite hard to answer that. I want to tell good stories but there are so many layers in every story I write that clearly I have other motivations as well. Justice is a huge theme with me, I'm very keen on justice. Also truth, what is truth? How do you define truth? I'm not a believer in absolute truth, and I think that the first and foremost absolute truth is the existence of God. I'm an atheist and if you don't believe, then you start to question truth in every sphere and very specifically when you're writing a crime novel. The thinking in the '30s, '40s and '50s with crime writers such as Margery Allingham, Agatha Christie, Dorothy L. Sayers, was that you had certain characters who were believable and trustworthy, usually in the shape of the series detective. You could always believe Miss Marple for example, and that what she said was true. My work has moved very far away from that. I have no characters you can believe at the beginning of a book. I set out very deliberately to destabilise them because when a policeman goes on to the scene of a crime in real life he has to disbelieve everybody. That element of truth and certainty fascinates me greatly and it's certainly one of the motivations behind each of the books.

You went to a rather genteel boarding school for girls. Did it shape your outlook?

Well yes I think very much so. It was High Church. I have

to say rather sadly I rejected God at school I think because of the very High Church element of it. It's where I understood how important people were in my life and very specifically I understood the importance of friends, the support you had from people who loved you. And that has always been a very important part of life. I think love is so important. My belief in redemption is all to do with love. It really doesn't matter whether you believe in the redemption of God's love or whether you believe in human love for redemption. In some cases learning to love yourself is a form of redemption. Certainly I learnt all that at school, it was a very loving environment looking back on it.

So you've logged friendship as one of your moral imperatives?

Yes. I believe the truth of Donne's 'no man is an island' argument. Yet I write about dysfunctional families, because I've always seen the family as either the most supportive unit in society, the one you can always rely on when all else fails, or the most damaging and most destructive. When it doesn't work it fails spectacularly and the damage done to children from within homes where there is no love – or the love is not shown properly and there is abuse, anger, violence, screaming, shouting – can be enormous.

Children of course can be wounded by random events and when you were nine your father died. That had a profound effect on you.

I think at the time – this is such an awful thing to say – at the time the effect it had on me was embarrassment. I remember the awful embarrassment of everybody knowing, people being extra nice to me because they didn't know how to deal with it. And all you wanted was to sink back into the flow of things, not to be singled out. You feel very guilty about that as you get older. You think 'My goodness, I've put my feelings way above what is an absolute tragedy.' And the grief is delayed. In fact I didn't feel any real grief until my children were born and then I was absolutely overwhelmed with grief for the loss of my father. Death has a very strange impact on children I think, and it does make you question yourself as you grow older. You question how honest your own feelings are about anything.

When your family suffered the loss of your father, your mother was left with three children. Was it a struggle?

Yes. We were lucky in one respect, that we were all bright enough to get scholarships to boarding schools because Ma was finding it completely impossible to look after us at home when we were all at different schools. I was a very early latchkey kid because my mother was working. Because she worried about us coming home to an empty house, that's why we went to boarding school. We ended up all three of us having a very fine education which we probably would not have had, had my father not died. In a sense that provides another guilt trip. I was aware that certain good things happened to me as a result of my father's death. And that still troubles me.

Come adolescence and you abandon God as taught to you by your Anglican boarding school. Did you put anything in its place? Did you seek answers?

I think I realised probably by the time I got to university that I didn't need answers or that there were no answers. The closest analogy I can offer is that I look out the window and I can accept the eternity of the universe, in other words, I don't need to put a box round the universe. I don't need to say this is the universe, it's in a box, what's on the other side of the wall? If you can accept that sort of eternity, then I can accept the eternity of man or the eternity of nature. If I was to put anything in the place of God I suppose I would put natural elements. I do have a belief that the earth will go on. Man makes his own fate and either we are responsible in what we do or we are not. The planet will continue until the sun burns out. I can accept that as a belief. Man does need to understand that he is responsible for himself and his environment and his future.

The former Archbishop of Canterbury, George Carey has written that the lot of the atheist is a deep and barren world of total bleakness.

No, no I think it's so much more comfortable to be an atheist. I mean I always liked the Diderot saying when he was dying and his friends came rushing in and said 'Look, you really must confess to the priest now. Come back to the Church, confess.' And he said 'No, because if God exists he will not blame me for being wrong.' And I have always felt that to be true. I mean if God is, as he is described in many religions, honest, then he isn't going to condemn me for being wrong. As long as I have striven to lead the best life that I can in terms of not being unkind to people, not deliberately setting out to destroy other people, I will not be condemned.

You don't think a moral code needs to be underpinned by some sort of supernatural legitimisation?

Absolutely not. To my mind, the best moral code that's ever been offered is Christ's moral code – love God, love thy neighbour. Now I can't do the loving God bit but I certainly think loving your neighbour is an important rule that we should all live by. I've had some neighbours I haven't liked very much but I think you never set out to deliberately harm somebody.

You're a great story-teller yourself. What do you make of the narrative stories in the Bible?

Oh, I think they're wonderful. I had such good grounding in the Bible because of the school I went to that my knowledge is quite large. It does worry me that I talk to youngsters today who actually have not had much of an introduction to the Bible. It think it's very important that we should all read it because you can only reject something, you can only say I am an atheist if you understand what it is you are rejecting.

So you can reject religion for yourself, but you're in favour of religious education?

Yes, because I think you need to understand what God stands for and what some people believe he is. I would love to have been instructed in the Koran, Buddhism. I'd love to have had a wide religious education. I've read some. But I do see them as stories and I think this is the distinction between me and a believer. I see them as fables beautifully written with some factual basis, in fact in some instances quite a lot of factual basis. But because I know how to construct a story, I read Matthew, Mark, Luke and John (not so much John but the first three), and I can see the common root. We can all see that they're working from a common script while putting their own flavour on the way they write. Everybody has a different style. I don't question Jesus' existence at all, I think he was a very fine man and I have huge admiration for him. My problem is making that leap from Jesus to God because the Trinity seems to me a very bizarre concept.

Many non-believers hedge their bets by saying that they're agnostic.
You have the courage to say, no, I'm an atheist.

Absolutely. I have never complained when anybody else changes their mind about something, so were I to change my mind I would feel that was an honourable thing to do. As things are at the moment I cannot believe in any being other than humanity here on earth. I wish there were more like me because when you realise that there is nobody to make it better, you know you cannot pray, you cannot appeal for intercession from somebody who can correct things, I think you have to correct them yourself. When I go into prison as a prison visitor I have long chats with the prisoners on this very subject because most of them can't believe in God or don't believe in God. And if I challenge them about the fact that this is their only life and unless they correct it now they will never have another chance because there is nothing better waiting somewhere else, they do start to think about responsibility. It's an existentialist argument but it works sometimes with them. They do actually begin to think.

Where do good and evil come from?

Well I do not believe in evil as a force in life and I don't believe that people are evil. I think we can perform evil acts. I don't dispute that for one moment. I think the humanity of people, whatever they've done – and I've spoken to many murderers – they still have a humanity which is often very accessible and very charming in some instances. It's frightening, even shocking sometimes to meet a murderer and discover a very human person behind the 'animal' that the tabloids have described.

Let's talk then about the world of your imagination, violent, cruel deeds. Are you familiar with death yourself?

Well you know the funny thing is I've been asked this before and I said, yes, we all are. I do believe that sleep is the little death and I'm never afraid to go to sleep at night. I actually I look forward to it. I cannot believe that death is so different. I think particularly if you've suffered a painful illness I think the long sleep is something you really look forward to. But where do I get these often quite lurid and horrible crimes from? They really are imagination but based on a lot of reading. I've built up a large reference library, and I have a good memory of what I've read so I'm simply tapping into that. People ask me, though, why are your murders always so brutal? It is to shock people. The murders are always at the beginning of my books because I want to remind people that I am about to tell them a story about the ultimate theft, the worst crime anybody can ever commit, taking somebody else's life which you can never replace. There is no real atonement for murder. Yes the crime genre is entertainment, but I want to say to everybody it is also shocking, horrible. This is what happens when violent death, premature violent death, occurs.

Do you sense that you have a dark side and indeed if you didn't assuage it by writing the books, what would you do with it?

It's worrying, isn't it! Psychological profiles of serial killers point out that they become addicted to fantasy and use all sorts of imagery to bolster their fantasies. Eventually they get to the point where the fantasies are not enough and they have to start acting them out which is why they start killing. And I have to say, yes, I do worry occasionally that because I do have this very vivid imagination and it does dwell on these sorts of issues, I am living with disturbed people in my head for the length of time it takes to write the book. And I'm thinking to myself where does all this come from? Is it catharsis? Am I working out on the page what I might do in real life? I have to say I don't think so!

You are a regular prison visitor and have acquaintance with criminals. Does this also represent an encounter with evil of some kind?

Well no. Eleven years ago before I started prison visiting I did believe in evil, but having spent 11 years visiting prisons, I don't any more. I have spoken to too many people who have committed all sorts of different crimes and some very bad crimes. And I find I cannot describe them as evil. It has quite changed my perceptions of life. What I've come to understand is that humanity is really quite a frail thing, that we are all capable under certain circumstances of doing things that we deeply and utterly regret. But murderers and rapists can never make better what they've done and that is something they have to live with and it's not easy to do. I've seen people crucified by remorse for what they've done. You can only see that when you go in and talk to them. I think it's important that as many of us as possible understand what doing something beyond taboos does to us.

There are people such as Myra Hindley, the Wests, Peter Sutcliffe, the killers of Jamie Bulger – who are simply referred to by the popular press and popular opinion as vile monsters. What's your view of them?

No, I think what they've done is beyond humanity. I have a problem with the killers of Jamie Bulger simply because they were so young that I'm not sure how possible it is at the age of 10 to fully comprehend what it is you're doing. I absolutely do not condone anything any of these people have done. And I would not seek to let them off punishment. Justice is the bedrock on which democracies are founded. And if you commit a crime that goes against all the rules of society and all the ethical views in society then you certainly have to pay a penalty. That means going to prison for however long you should be there.

All I'm saying is that just as I am a different person now from the one I was at 19, and very specifically I'm a different person now from the one I was at 10, I think we need to allow people to seek redemption for themselves even if it means they have to do that within the prison environment – possibly forever. But the idea that we, society, can dictate who may be redeemed and who may not is wrong.

So this division in the popular imagination between evil monsters and the rest of us, you don't accept the division?

No. I would go along with the description of some of the worst crimes as being deeply evil, but not that the perpetrators were monsters. What I'm trying to argue here is that nobody remains static. They are not likely to remain the same person as they were at the moment that they committed an evil act. They are not likely to remain as that person for the next 20 years. And because we don't have capital punishment, because we say we will not judicially murder you as a punishment, but instead put you in prison for the length of time that is set, then within that period you will have the opportunity to become a better person. That to me is what we should be doing. That's what society is about, to say to people, 'Yes this was despicable, and because we live in a decent civilised society we will give you the chance to atone in whatever way you can.'

But if you don't believe in God or religion as a source of redemption, where is redemption to come from? How is it brought about?

Purely through contact with people, which is why I'm a great advocate of prison visiting. I think a prison visitor, merely by being somebody from outside who offers the hand of friendship to somebody who needs it, plays an important role. I think friendship is this beginning of salvation. It demonstrates that you are not so dreadful, you are not so evil and so reviled that nobody will hold out a hand to you.

Do you think that the prison system is the only way of treating crime or do you think we will evolve other systems?

I find it very bizarre that 150 years after prisons, the Victorian prisons, were built we're still dealing with crime in almost exactly the same way. I have a lot of question marks over how we deal with criminal behaviour. My first and foremost feeling is that you ignore at your peril the way that people live. If you create sink estates for example, I think you can only expect people living in deprived conditions, particularly the youngsters, to follow the route of crime. Truancy is one of my biggest bugbears. We must not allow children to truant from school because the moment you start truanting, and drop out of formal education, you make so many problems for yourself.

You speak about justice and your concern about dysfunctional families. So you probably have your own rather strong sense of personal morality.

Yes, I think I have very strong moral values for myself. There are things I will do and things I won't do. It might not be a morality that's necessarily recognisable to other people but I do believe in living by principle. You take somebody like Thomas More or Archbishop Cranmer you look at their morality, things they were prepared to die for. It's that great conundrum, isn't it? If you'd been in the French Resistance would you have given away the names of your cell under torture? And you never know the answer. I'd like to believe I'd go to my death for my principles.

You say that you have those principles for yourself and you believe in them. I know you strive not to be judgmental but do you endorse a common morality?

Yes I do and I would endorse almost any religious code of ethics. The Ten Commandments is a very sensible and workable social code. But my principles are largely to do with truth. For example, I don't tell lies and I get very angry with people who do. I think it's inexcusable. Now the truth isn't always pleasant but I think it's important. The people I trust are the ones who tell the truth. I don't trust people who don't tell the truth and I think trust is very important. So I suppose my principles are all along the lines of loyalty, honesty and truth.

�֍

16

JOHN TAVENER

'Primordial depth'

John Tavener was composing music at school. By the age of 25 he was Professor of Music Composition at Trinity College of Music in London. In 1968 his Cantata, The Whale, *was premiered at the Proms and recorded on the Beatles' Apple label. Since then there has been a steady outpouring of primarily religious music. His* Song for Athene *was sung at the funeral of Princess Diana;* The Protecting Veil, *written for cellist Steven Isserlis in 1989, had universal success. And it was his music –* A New Beginning *– that hailed the millennium year at London's Dome. His commitment to religious music is at one with his faith, for many years to the Eastern Orthodox Church but more recently taking a broader perspective. Since 2001, he has looked for inspiration to a metaphysic that embraces all the great religions:* The Veil of the Temple, Lament for Jerusalem *uses both Christian and Islamic texts;* Hymn of Dawn *embraces Hindu, Sufi, Christian and Jewish texts; and* The Beautiful Names *celebrates the 99 names of God according to the Islamic tradition.*

Music should be liquid metaphysics. If it is not that, if it doesn't express love, if it doesn't express some kind of metaphysics, then for me it's not doing anything at all.

Lennox Berkeley used to tell me that you have to find your

own voice. I now see that's ridiculous. You don't have to find your own voice, you have to find the primordial voice. And one spends one's whole life looking for this primordial voice.

And where is it?

I find it in all sorts of places. I live in Dorset now for instance and I live next to a very beautiful hill, an ancient Celtic burial site and I find since I've been living here that the logos, as it were, the logos of God is expressed not just in Jesus of Nazareth, that's terribly narrow, but it's also expressed in virgin nature and I find nowadays, I walk sometimes for three or four hours a day in virgin nature and while I'm walking in nature, I suppose not in a conventional way but in a strange way, I pray. And when I come back I'm full of melodies and I write them out. And we have to return to this simple approach to music to understand that there is a primordial depth that ancient man understood but modern man has totally lost.

A lot of Western music is art for art's sake. It's written according to a formula. It's not really connected to the root in us. It doesn't have its connection in virgin nature. It doesn't have its connection in going towards the centre which is God. It seems to have its connection on the periphery and one hears so much of it, peripheral sounds in the modern day.

It seems your music has always been identified with your faith. You grew up in a Presbyterian home and were writing music for the Presbyterian Church by the age of 14.

I can remember even as a child of three that I had a maternal grandfather who was very receptive to my improvising on the piano, the sounds of nature, the sounds of lightning, the sounds of rain, of thunderstorms. So at a very early age I was already involved with a kind of belief. Having come to Dorset

I've moved back closer to that, the thing I felt when I was three, by embracing virgin nature and realising that it is also a manifestation of God. Recently I have a feeling of distance from the organised Church. In fact I distance myself totally and I don't go to church.

Your Church told you a narrative story of Jesus, his disciples, his death on the cross and the Resurrection. Did you simply accept these stories?

I don't know that it was a personal acceptance. It's a strange thing, faith. For instance when I was young I had a real crush on Igor Stravinsky. I remember asking my mother to take me to all his rehearsals at the BBC. But now I see it's not the music of Stravinsky that interests me, but the fact that he was Orthodox. I made myself love the music but I only realised recently that I don't really love the music. He's as much a modernist as Picasso, for instance. But I found that because he was Russian Orthodox, what he had to say about that interested me. So the fact that I became Orthodox much later at the age of about 30, was already present in the fact that I had this young person's crush on Stravinsky.

Did you realise at the time he was Orthodox?

Yes I did. I did. I wanted to know everything about him. Stravinsky was not a mystical character, not remotely. But it was a side of him that I think he never fully came to terms with. That's why his music always remains modernist and doesn't touch me at the really deep centre.

What about your parents, were they devout?

I wouldn't say they were devout. No. My grandparents were rather strict. They liked to be in church in their pew on

Sunday mornings, the best pew. My grandfather, I remember, during one of the sermons, got out his gold watch and started to make uncomfortable noises because the sermon had been going on too long.

Music took hold very early, didn't it? Was it already associated then with something beyond notes and harmonies?

I think it always was. In some of the early things I did like a setting of the creed, I wanted to embrace some kind of tradition. All through my teenage years I always wrote music that was religious in intent. I can't explain it any other way. I can feel the notes. I sort of feel it in my body when I'm walking in Dorset. I can feel the notes welling up in my body. I can tell whether they're right by looking at virgin nature, because in a sense virgin nature is God's art. This is what the narrowness of Christianity doesn't comprehend. It's not just the revelation of Jesus of Nazareth. Everywhere you look is God, if you look for it in the right places. You wander in nature. You're in his nature.

Now let's talk about what's called your 'hippie period' when you wrote The Whale *and had a big success with it. Were you ambitious? What worldly success did you seek?*

I think maybe in those days I drank far too much. Nowadays I don't drink at all. But I'm sure I did in those early days. And it was wonderful, I must say, to be alive in the '60s. I enjoyed myself, and although I never got involved with drugs, I enjoyed that certain kind of life. You had people like the Beatles, like John Cage, all of them were fascinating. I'm very glad I knew the Beatles. John Lennon and Yoko Ono always played me their tapes, and I played them my tapes. Everyone one met, one met for a purpose, to move somewhere else, then to move somewhere else, and move somewhere else again. One's always moving somewhere else until in the end one leaves everybody and is left alone with God.

Did the '60s offer a liberating sense of ideas?

Oh, yes, it did. I was slightly angry in those days. *The Whale* has a certain angry young man sound to it. And I made an opera on Jean Genêt's *Notre Dame Des Fleurs*. That was a pretty extraordinary subject because his concept of religion was basically by blaspheming. And in the Presbyterian church where I played the organ, I gave out sheets of music of this highly blasphemous text. I got this Presbyterian choir full of very strait-laced Scottish ladies to sing the most astonishing things. Though the piece never finally took life, I'm amazed that I got them to do it.

Do you think this was the rite of passage of a young man?

I found success difficult, and I felt I needed to withdraw a bit, to work out spiritually where my orientation was. Clearly I couldn't have gone on just being an organist in a Presbyterian church, have a choir of old Scottish ladies. I withdrew and I met at that time a young Roman Catholic girl who had worked in Mexico and whom I fell in love with. She gave me a Mexican cross and said she was in love with me, but she was also going into a convent and of course, this tore my life to shreds. Looking back on it, it was an enormous step towards faith of some kind. Because of her I became interested in the Spanish mystic St John of the Cross who always expressed his love of God through the erotic, but transfiguring the erotic. I was able to write an enormous piece called *Ultimos Ritos*. She was the vehicle through whom I was able to write it. I realise now the reason I had to meet this person.

And in the end you chose the Eastern Orthodox Church. Was this a sudden decision?

I became somewhat afraid of the Roman Catholic Church. I was conscious of a desire to convert me, whereas the Orthodox Church took a different view. If one compares my dealing with a priest at Westminster Cathedral who was saying things like, 'Now, John, I think the Lord wants you.' Well that made me run a mile. Metropolitan Anthony of the Russian Orthodox, when I told him what my life was like, that it was not very good, and I wanted to join the Orthodox Church, he said 'No, no, no. You're not ready.' I thought, 'This is wonderful. I'm interested in this Church because they're not really interested in me.'

You had always been particularly close to your mother?

Yes, very close. I felt I couldn't leave home until she died, which is true. I didn't leave home until I was 40 because I felt instinctively I could never leave until she died.

When she died you said you couldn't write any more music.

That's true. I felt that I needed to be near to help her die. I seriously thought I could help her die. She'd given me so much. She'd taken me to see Stravinsky when I was young. She'd put up with the fact that I was extremely difficult. She was the one who really championed my music. I somehow needed to be there when she died. In point of fact, when it came to it, I suddenly realised this woman's astonishingly strong. She said to my father 'You've got to remarry'. 'And as for you,' she said to me, 'you must get married too.' She said 'I don't want to talk about it. I shall miss you all. I shall miss the grandchildren.' It was when she became in charge of the whole thing, I suddenly realised that in her quiet way she had probably been in control of everything.

It felt terribly important that an Orthodox priest be present at her actual death. So I contacted Father Michael. He came and read the Orthodox last rites over her. And I had the most wonderful gift. It seemed sent from heaven. The moment he said 'Amen', she died.

The remark about not writing any more music now she was dead, seems to fly in the face of her wishes for you.

After she died I went to Greece. It was a country I always went to. She loved Greece too. I went to Greece and I was alone with nature. I wandered around on a Greek island and I remember thinking I'll never write anything again. But then I started looking at this poem by Kalvos, who was a Greek poet. And I knew he'd written an Ode to Death. And it was about the death of my mother. And suddenly ideas started to come. And I prayed over the relics of St Nektarios of Aegina, and I put my head next to his skull and remember hearing 'Where your treasure is there will your heart be also.' And I went out feeling totally changed, feeling it was possible for me to write music. And it just poured out. From that time onwards it has simply poured out, non stop.

Some time after that you met another strong woman, Mother Thekla. How did she change things for you?

She changed things for me because she produced a kind of wildness, almost as if I'd been looking for someone like her. She was a person who'd fallen out with almost every kind of authority in the Orthodox Church. She had become in a sense a loner, living with a small group of hermit nuns in the wilds of the Yorkshire Moors. I'd read what she'd written about Mary of Egypt, about Shakespeare. I think I knew her for about four years before I met her.

And did she influence the music?

Oh, yes. Enormously. She made me understand what tradition was. Not changing guards at Buckingham Palace, but something much deeper than that. It was a question of finding music that was already there. It was a question of being in touch with a force that was beyond ourselves. Of course, being an abbess she had to toe the party line at times but she's always been a wild person and totally unpredictable. I saw her recently and she's beginning to look like the Yorkshire Moors herself. I think it's wonderful that I met this person, this primal force.

What did you find in the Orthodox Church different from the Western Church, that mattered to you?

I think it was their comprehension of tradition and their comprehension of nature. One thinks of the early desert fathers, in particular the Egyptian fathers. They have a marvellous sense of God being everywhere. And they have a sense of what primordial tradition is. I think if I have to define what I've been looking for, it is to understand the primordial.

Can we unpack the word 'primordial' a little? What do you understand by it?

Only a week ago a holy man from the Apache tribe of American Indians came here and he brought me a wonderful pow-wow drum at which four Indians sit. And they beat it and it makes the most astonishing primordial sound. I invited him to stay for supper. He was young, extremely beautiful-looking with very long hair right down his back. But he had a sort of gravitas, a kind of ancient look, and I would say he looked intensely primordial. I want to describe the evening because it gets near to what I mean by the word. He went into our dining room where there's a huge icon of Christ. He turned towards it, then he raised his palm in American Indian fashion and over the food that was in front of him, he gave thanks to the fish who had yielded its life from the animal kingdom. He then turned to the vegetables with his palm again, and gave thanks to mother earth who had given us the vegetables. Then he raised his palm very solemnly and asked for the Great Spirit – which for Indians means God – to bless us. And I was very moved. If I have to describe primordial, that whole evening was primordial. Even more so, when I went to bed and could not sleep and after two hours I had a kind of vision where I saw Christ, where I saw the Mother of God, where I saw him, this Indian holy man with the pow-wow drum. He told me that I ought to play it and stroke it as he did, giving thanks to the animal – in this case an elk – that had given its skin. He said you must play rhythms on it and it will speak to you.

In the course of this week I have written about 60 pages of a new piece of music and it has been revealed to me through the drum. That's what I mean by primordial.

So we're way beyond church hierarchies and such?

I'm afraid we are. Up to this present time it has been through Christ that I've understood what God is. But one has to be careful that Christians don't take a totally exclusive view. What I find is that I can't enter Christian buildings without feeling that there is a misconception of what the revelation of the logos is. For Christians it was Christ. But the logos has revealed itself in other ways to other people. Living at the time we do, we have to understand there are other revelations of God: the revelation of Hinduism, the revelation of Buddhism, the revelation given to the prophet of Islam and the revelation of virgin nature to the American Indians. We have so much to learn from all of them.

Now there's a writer who's had a bigger influence on me than almost anyone in my life. That is Frithjof Schuon who was a Sufi master. I think he was the greatest metaphysician who ever lived. His writings are able to embrace Hinduism, Buddhism, Judaism, Christianity. He adored the American Indians which is why I'm convinced he's guiding me in some way now.

Intervening in your life from beyond the grave?

Yes. I see him in visions. Maybe I'm crackers but I see him and I see him as a young man. He's smiling, yet all his pictures show him as very fierce.

These people of whom we've spoken, Mother Thekla, the American Indian, the Sufi mystic, they're all a long way from Stravinsky, aren't they? Do you feel you've arrived at the end of a long journey?

I feel that I now have to write about the Sophia Perennis – that is the all-embracing nature of someone like Schuon or the Sufis in general who accept all religions. I'm very grateful to the Indian chief who brought me the pow-wow drum because if I listen hard enough, I will find the way to do it.

In the popular imagination you're known as the composer of the Song of Athene *sung at the funeral of Princess Diana.*

Yes, I was terribly impressed by seeing so many English people coming with candles and lighting candles. I thought this is not what English people do. There must be something primordial that happened ... there's that word again. I thought, 'What are they doing in tears? They're getting in touch with their primordial selves.' I don't think it was her personally they were grieving. They were grieving something else inside themselves. They were allowing themselves to be moved, to be deeply upset by what had happened.

You speak of visions, of people speaking to you from beyond. What is waiting beyond?

Perhaps 'beyond' is the wrong word. I just feel there is no such thing as death. There's only life. One sees examples of it in the Revelation of Christ. He showed there was no death, only life. All great holy men, in any tradition, say the same thing. One looks at nature, particularly now in spring, one looks at a flower which, having died, now shows its face towards the sun. There isn't any death. It's all life.

And the body?

We're just inside a mortal shell for a period of time. We shed it.

17

RICHARD DAWKINS

'In a sense humans have emancipated themselves from natural selection.'

It may seem odd that Richard Dawkins is included in an anthology of Belief, since he has such a reputation as a fierce critic of formal religions and their supernatural credos. But as one of science's most innovative thinkers he has his own world view of how and why the world is as it is. His first book The Selfish Gene *made a huge impact when it was first published in 1976. Other books with beguiling titles have offered further commentaries upon Darwin's concept of Natural Selection:* The Blind Watchmaker, River Out of Eden, Climbing Mount Improbable, Unweaving the Rainbow *and most recently* A Devil's Chaplain. *His book* The Extended Phenotype *is his most serious scientific work, his biggest claim to scientific innovation. He has been honoured by both science and literature, being awarded the Michael Faraday Prize by the Royal Society, and a Fellowship by the Royal Society of Literature.*

My decision to be a scientist was a bit of a drift really. I preferred biology to any other subject, but it was wasn't really until my second year as an undergraduate at Oxford that I really became deeply enthusiastic about science and about biology.

What about your faith? You were part of an orthodox Anglican home. Did it impinge very much on your life?

Not much. My parents were orthodox Anglican in the sense that they were both baptised, as was I. But they were not deeply religious. We used to go to church every Christmas, but I mean apart from that there wasn't a lot of it about.

You weren't confirmed?

I was confirmed. That was school influence. I was confirmed at my prep school at the age of 13 and when I was being confirmed, I did have a fairly active fantasy life about a relationship with God. I used to pray and I used to have fantasies about creeping down to the chapel in the middle of the night, and having blinding visions and things. I don't know really how seriously I took that.

How seriously do you take it now?

Well it was a fantasy, which happened in my head. It's not surprising that it should have happened because I was at that time being filled with all that sort of stuff in confirmation classes.

A nourishing fantasy?

I don't think so, no. I don't think it was at all a nourishing fantasy. I don't think it did me much harm, but I don't think it did me any good either.

You've written since about how much you disapprove of children being assigned the religion of their parents.

I do disapprove very strongly of labelling children, especially young children, as 'Catholic children' or 'Protestant children' or 'Islamic children'. That does seem to me to be very wicked because what you're in effect doing is making the assumption that the beliefs, the cosmology, the beliefs about the world, about life, are automatically going to be inherited in a way that you don't assume for anything else. And you certainly don't assume that a child will inherit his father's sports team, or love of ornithology, or politics.

Of course in practice, children very often do. You very often find that a child will in effect be influenced by a parent to take up bird watching or stamp collecting, that of course is absolutely fine. But society simply assumes, without even asking, that there is such a thing as a Catholic four-year-old, or a Muslim four-year-old. And that I do think is wicked.

Well you were, of course, automatically an Anglican. But confirmed at 13, read Darwin at 16…

Yes, that was a big leap for me, because by the time I reached the age of 16, I had lost all religious faith, with the exception of possibly a lingering feeling about the argument from design. So I'd already worked out that there are lots of different religions, and they contradict each other so they can't all be right. I was left with a sort of feeling of 'Oh well, there must be *some* sort of designer, some sort of spirit which designed the universe and designed life.' And it was when I understood Darwin that I saw how totally wrong that point of view was, that rather suddenly the scales fell from my eyes. I became rather strongly anti-religious at that point.

You went to Oxford in the early '60s. By the late '60s you were in California – and we're talking of the decade of student tumult.

Yes, and I got pretty much involved in it. It was at the height of Vietnam war resistance and most of the students and indeed most of the faculty at the University of California at Berkeley were against the war in Vietnam. I got pretty heavily involved in all of that.

And did that sway your view of what you now believe the world to be about?

I don't think in itself, no. Over the recent war in Iraq, I've come back to being fairly active in the same kind of direction. But I don't think that the experience in Berkeley particularly influenced me in that direction.

And then the books started arriving: and you give them very poetic titles: in 1976 you published The Selfish Gene, Blind Watchmaker *1986,* River Out of Eden *and* Unweaving the Rainbow, A Devil's Chaplain. *But what is interesting about* The Selfish Gene *is 'selfish' is a judgmental word. You're saying that the gene is behaving in a way that actually we don't think is a good thing. It carries that resonance.*

It certainly does. It carries that resonance, I'm not sure it carries a very poetic resonance which I think *The Blind Watchmaker* does, and I think *River Out of Eden*, which of course is just lifted straight from Genesis, so it's not surprising that's poetic. And *Unweaving the Rainbow* is lifted from Keats.

So, the writer is evolving along with the scientist, a literary sensibility running parallel with your wish to be clear about scientific ideas.

Yes, I do have a very, very strong desire to be clear. I really, really want my meaning to be understood by my readers. You'd think that was obvious, I mean, how could any writer not want to be understood? But you'd be surprised how many people do not actually want to be understood at all but, I regret to say, want to create some sort of an impression.

And the books for lay people of course have brought you a huge audience, an interest in what you yourself believe. Let's go through the different concepts that often arise in religious discourse: 'the purpose of life' – are you satisfied that you understand the purpose of life?

Well 'purpose' is a difficult word, and it's much misunderstood. As humans with consciousness, we have purposes which we actually visualise in our minds and we see in our mind's eye something that we wish to achieve. We're looking into the future, and attempting to achieve something. 'Purpose' is used by biologists in a very different way, but the resemblance comes because the products of Darwinian natural selection look so stunningly as though they have been designed for a purpose. And so something like a wing or a foot or an eye really does carry the most incredibly powerful illusion of purpose. Since Darwin we've understood where that illusion comes from, but it's such a strong illusion that it's almost impossible to resist using the language of purpose. So biologists will very often as a kind of shorthand say 'The purpose of a bird's wing is to fly.'

Where then does the concept of human purpose come from? There must be something within the human psyche.

Well there clearly is, and it's clearly a very strong part of our psyche. And I of course as a Darwinian would see it as yet another thing that has evolved. So just as we've evolved sexual desire, just as we've evolved hunger, we have also evolved a sense of purpose. And the sense of purpose in our wild ancestors would've been hugely useful because you can imagine a purpose of setting out on a hunt, a purpose of looking for a water hole, a purpose of finding a new camp site for the band to move to. Those are all very useful things, and the human brain was, I don't doubt, selected by Darwinian selection to develop this sense of purpose.

Was the human brain selected to develop religion?

I don't know, but my guess is no. The way I would answer that question is to say that the human brain was selected to develop something which manifests itself as religion under some circumstances. Let me explain what I mean by that. If I take an analogy of – one that I'm particularly fond of – the tendency of moths to fly into candle flames. It's tempting to label that suicidal behaviour in moths, and ask what on earth is the Darwinian advantage of suicidal behaviour in moths? If you put it like that, clearly there isn't any. But if you say instead 'What is the Darwinian survival value of having the kind of brain which under some circumstances leads moths to fly into candle flames?' Then you're getting somewhere, because then you can say 'Well in the world where moths evolved, there weren't any candle flames. The only lights you would see if you were a night-flying moth would be things like the moon and the stars, and they are an optical infinity, which means that their rays are coming parallel. And if you have a rule of thumb in your brain that says "Steer a steady angle of say 30 degrees to the rays of the moon", that's a very useful thing to do, because that keeps you going in a dead straight line. That rule of thumb is then misapplied to candles, which are not at optical infinity, where the rays are radiating outwards. And if you follow the same rule of thumb, of keeping an angle of 30 degrees to the candle's rays, then you'll simply spiral into the candle and burn yourself.' So it's wrong to ask 'Why do moths fly

211

into candle flames?' The right question is 'Why do they have the kind of brain which in the wild state made them do something which in the human-dominated state where there are candles, makes them fly into candle flames?'

Now in the case of religion, I think there was something built into the human brain by natural selection, which was once useful and which now manifests itself under civilised conditions as religion, but which used not to be religion when it first arose, and when it was useful.

Well, given that religion arises in most cultures, do you believe that there are benefits of solidarity, tribal unity, mutual generosity, within religions, that are useful to those communities?

Yes, there very possibly are. I should qualify that by saying that as a Darwinian, usefulness to communities is not what it's about. Darwinism is about usefulness to individuals, or rather their genes, to be more precise. So usefulness to communities is an added benefit. But benefit or not, I don't think that's why it evolved. I think that's a kind of incidental bonus.

Let's talk about the three-letter word – God. You don't believe in God. What is interesting is how the use of the word varies now. Many people use it in a Sunday school sense, but some people including scientists, are using it in a more abstract sense.

Yes, Einstein frequently used the word 'God' in very clearly what was not a 'Sunday school' way. It's not entirely clear from his statements what he meant by it. It was somewhere between deism, the belief that some sort of intelligence started the universe going and then stepped back and did nothing else, which actually I don't think Einstein believed, and a sort of pantheism, where he was using the word 'God' as just a name for the laws of nature, the laws of physics, for which he had a deep reverence, as do I.

So would you call the laws of physics 'God'?

No, I don't think it's helpful to do so. Einstein clearly would. I think it was unfortunate that he did so, because many people whose idea of God is a 'Sunday school' idea of God think that Einstein was meaning that too, which he very clearly wasn't. It deeply irritated him when he was so misunderstood. I think Einstein would've done much better never to have used the word 'God', then he would not have been misunderstood.

Stephen Hawking talks about 'The mind of God'.

Stephen Hawking ends his famous book by saying 'Then we would know the mind of God.' That's precisely like Einstein. Stephen Hawking was looking forward to a day when physicists would finally unify all their theories and understand everything, and 'Then we should know the mind of God' was a poetic way of expressing that. Neither Stephen Hawking nor Einstein believe in a personal God.

What does the poet in you make of the use of the word 'God'?

Well, I think it's a legitimate, poetic device and I wouldn't mind doing it in the way that Einstein and Hawking have done, but for the fact that it is so eagerly misunderstood. There are just thousands of people out there who desperately want people like Einstein and Hawking to believe in the kind of personal God who forgives sins and listens to prayers, and gives you comfort when you're bereaved. And because there is that deep hunger out there to believe in that kind of God, I think that Einstein and Hawking do a disservice by using the word 'God'. I think it misleads people.

So which is the God you don't believe in?

I certainly don't believe in a God who answers prayers, forgives sins, listens to misfortunes, cares about your sins, cares about your sex life, makes you survive death, performs miracles – that is most certainly a God I don't believe in. Einstein's God, which simply means the laws of nature which are so deeply mysterious that they inspire a feeling of reverence – I believe in that, but I wouldn't call it God.

What about Buddhism, mysticism, contemplation, meditation?

I know little about Buddhism but meditation as a kind of mental discipline to manipulate your mind in beneficial directions, I could easily imagine. Reciting trance-inducing phrases could even be beneficial ... but it certainly has nothing whatever to do in my mind with a belief in anything supernatural.

Do scientists have to have something that they might call 'faith'?

I would prefer not to call it 'faith'. There are times when scientists have a deep conviction that they're right, and that drives them to do more experiments. It never drives good scientists to their conclusions. What it does is drive them to decide to do more experiments, to do more research, to think further in a particular line rather than another line. There's also I suppose a faith in logic and rationality as something that works, and it's possible to play philosophical games and say that, that is in itself is a form of faith. There are I think rather bad philosophers, who attempt to say that that's only one of many viewpoints on life. But I've no patience

214

with philosophers who say that any belief is just as good as mine. It isn't.

And we're not far from the statement that science is just another kind of religion.

Exactly. And I find that a pernicious view. The difference is that science works.

Let's take another religious word – 'evil'. Do you have a concept of evil?

I mistrust the uses of words like 'evil'. I'm happy to use a word like 'evil' of a particular individual. I'm happy to say that 'Adolf Hitler was evil, Adolf Hitler did evil things.' But too many people leap to the conclusion 'Oh there must be some kind of evil spirit which entered into Hitler,' or 'There's a spirit of evil abroad.' That I think is unhelpful putting it mildly. And another phrase – 'the human spirit'? I am very suspicious of using of words like, 'spirit'. I'm happy to do so, as long as it doesn't suggest anything supernatural or ghostly. To say that something is explicable in terms of the brain, in terms of interactions between neurones, it is vitally important to understand and not reduce it. It is actually a far more wonderful explanation than just to say 'Oh it's the human spirit.' The human spirit explains nothing. You've said precisely nothing when you say it's the human spirit.

So are you saying that we undervalue, we haven't yet begun to celebrate what goes on in our head?

Exactly. We haven't begun to celebrate what goes on in our heads and what goes on in the world, what goes on in the universe. These are so much grander, so much more wildly exciting than whatever you can convey by a really rather trite phrase like 'the human spirit'. Again as a poetic phrase, I don't have a problem with it.

If you live in what you might call the mechanistic world of ideas, where do your values come from?

If by values you mean 'things that I think are worth striving for, things that I think are beautiful', those are all values.

Where does 'beauty' come from?

Well, I think beauty ultimately has to come from the way the brain is set up. The brain is a devastatingly complicated mechanism. We're only just beginning to understand how it works. And our response to certain things as 'beautiful' must be explicable ultimately in those terms. I hesitate to say that, because some people think that in some way that demeans it, which of course it doesn't. When I am moved to tears as I can be by the slow movement of a Schubert quartet, it is not in any sense to demean that experience, to say that there is nothing going on other than activity in my neurones.

Nonetheless it is one of the sublimest experiences, the experience of art. And there are people – not you – who have suggested that there is a scientific way of looking at the world, which runs parallel to say a religious way of looking at the world, or a poetic way of looking at the world. And in some way they all exist at the same time, but don't interrelate. What do you feel about that?

I don't really see how they could not interrelate.

Now you are a Darwinian, but in terms of politics and the world and how we live, you are an anti-Darwinian, because you do not believe in the survival of the fittest.

Well, I believe in the survival of the fittest as an explanation for the evolution of life. There have been people who have advocated the survival of the fittest as a kind of political creed, where they justify a form of right-wing politics or economics on the grounds that it conforms to the laws of nature. That I do object to, as indeed does any other modern Darwinian. We don't want to see Darwinism being used to justify things like fascism, which it has been.

So is Darwinism over now? Has natural selection come to an end?

Well, only in humans. Humans are just a very, very small part of the panoply of life, and it is arguable that in a certain sense, humans have emancipated themselves from Darwinian selection. But it's not over. Darwinism is still *the* explanation for the existence of all life, including ourselves, even if just at this moment, we're not indulging in Darwinism.

Has man then put a block on Darwinism in his own evolution?

If it were true that he has – and I'm not at all sure – the way it would come to be true is that we don't die young any more, or it's rather difficult to. That means that most people who want to reproduce do. In the past the people who reproduced would be those who made it. And so natural selection was a winnowing process – some survived, some didn't. The ones that survived reproduced and passed on the genes that made them survive. If we live in a welfare state where everybody survives, then there's not the same sense in which genes that make you survive are the ones that get passed on. Any old genes can get passed on, if the welfare state keeps you alive. That would be the point of view that somebody who said that … Darwinism had come to an end in humans. I'm not sure that I'm going to say that.

So what view do you take?

Well, I think there may be more subtle processes of selection going on. Clearly not everybody does reproduce. Some people reproduce a lot more than others. If there is any genetic component to the variants in reproductive success, the word 'success' being a neutral word, if you divide those people who have lots of children from those people who have none and then you ask the question 'Is there any statistical tendency for this lot to have a different set of genes statistically from that lot, then by definition, we've got natural selection going on. Of course it may be that that particular selection pressure is so short-lived in historical time, that it doesn't lead to any interesting evolution. I mean there could be a selection going on for example, in favour of incompetence in using contraceptives. I don't really believe that, but that gives you the idea of the kind of thing that might be going on.

So do you believe that the destiny of the human race is in its genes and is it something about which you are able to be optimistic or pessimistic?

Well I'm not sure I would say destiny is in the genes. As for optimism or pessimism, I'm open-minded. By temperament I suppose I'm optimistic, but that doesn't mean by intellect I am. I think one can separate those, and on a good day you can feel warm and optimistic. But if you actually think rationally about the future, then it may have a more pessimistic cast.

You're often described by the religious in our society as a scientific fundamentalist. Do you mind?

I do mind being called a fundamentalist. I think a fundamentalist is somebody who believes something unshakeably and isn't going to change their mind. Somebody who believes something because it's written in their holy book. I absolutely repudiate any suggestion that I am that. I would, like any other scientist, willingly change my mind if the evidence led me to do so. I care about what's true, I care about evidence, I care about evidence as the reason for knowing what is true. It is true that I come across rather passionate sometimes – that's because I am passionate about the truth.

18

ANDREW MOTION

'The value of the numinous'

Andrew Motion began publishing poetry in 1976. Since then his volumes of poetry have included The Pleasure Steamers, Natural Causes, Salt Water *and* Public Property. *He was made Poet Laureate in 1999. He is also the biographer of* The Lamberts *(1986),* Philip Larkin *(1993) and* Keats *(1998). He is a Fellow of the Royal Society of Literature and currently Professor of Creative Writing at Royal Holloway College, University of London.*

I believe that some of the things art has been able to do, and writing in particular, amounts to a kind of activity which runs parallel to more orthodox kinds of religious faith. That is to say: art can have consoling, therapeutic, salubrious, humanising values, in much the same way that orthodox religion can have. I don't mean that writers themselves are god-like. But there is something permanent in art which is compatible with the goal of religious faith.

So does that mean that you as a poet have something of the role that the priesthood once had for people without faith, that they look to you for the sort of truths about life that they once sought in the Church?

Well, that might be true. I think that before we go more deeply into it, we need to say that art makes a separation between its creator and itself in a way that priests probably don't feel they have to. The fact is that you might be the most appalling human being, and yet be able to write a wonderfully humane poem. As we cast our eye over literary history, we can see that on the whole, there is very little compatibility between excellent people and excellent work. On the other hand, we would expect priests to connect their life with their work. They would in that sense be exemplary people, as well as delivering an exemplary message.

Does that excuse you from leading or trying to lead an exemplary life?

Well, I try as well as I can, but I don't always succeed. In fact I often fail miserably. But I have made the separation between the person I am and the work that I produce, that is certainly true.

Did you grow up in a devout home?

Yes, I did. My father, who is still alive, is a devout Christian of an absolutely classic, Church of England kind. He lives in the countryside and he goes to church in the country village. My mother, who's been dead for a good long while now, also went to church in a regular way. She was seriously ill for the last 10 years of her life, and during that time big questions of faith mattered to her a great deal.

Before we come to that, because I know that was a major crisis in your life, let's speak of your unhappiness at school. You were sent away quite young to a very unhappy and fearful life at prep school where you said prayers at night and slept with your hand on the Bible. What did your belief amount to at that time?

I had a very crude idea of what faith was there for. I thought it was to help me in time of trouble. I reckoned that if I could somehow get God on my side, or make a direct appeal to him, he wouldn't let me down. He might make me do my Latin prep better so that I wouldn't get whacked. I had very elaborate rituals of worship. I used to say the Lord's Prayer seven times before falling asleep at night – somehow the idea had got into my head that seven was a lucky number. I felt that I was putting something in and therefore I might get something back.

Were your prayers answered?

Hard to say. I think I persuaded myself that they were, because by some semi-miraculous process term used to end and I would go home and be happier again. You can see this is all pretty low flying, philosophically speaking.

You've written of course a great deal about your mother who died so young and you spoke in one phrase of the idyll of her company. This relationship with your mother was particularly close and unclouded.

Yes, the influence of her personality was very strong on me. She was a very sweet-natured, kind, but also amusing and kind of up-for-life person. A very good mixture in fact, with a strong, moral structure to her life and a strong set of beliefs.

You were 17 when she had her terrible riding accident that left her three years in a coma, and then in a half-life limbo for another seven.

Yes, it was absolutely the defining thing for my life. Even though I'm now 48 and it's all a long time ago, I realise on a more or less daily basis that the things I think about life – how it is shaped, and what I expect from it – are almost all predicated on my experience during the 10 years of her illness. Essentially, it's to do with a notion of life's randomness. On bad days, that idea of randomness turns into something al-most malicious or malevolent – by which I mean that if life can give you a good kicking, it will. On normal days, I just think: you better look out because it will get you if it can.

Did you rail against your God for what had happened?

Yes. Up to the age or 16 or so, my religious beliefs were pretty simplistic. I'd been to this loathsome prep school which had very regular patterns of religious worship. I then went to a public school called Radley College, which had originally been an Oxford Movement foundation. It had a very clear religious structure, chapel every day, more extended worship on Sundays, and I was very interested in this. Sometimes I used to go more than once a day, in that swooning, obsessive way that adolescents can have. Then almost immediately after my mother's accident, I started to walk away from it. I thought, this is crazily unfair and a betrayal of all the things that I have believed in. I lost my faith in about a week, and at the end of the week I thought well, what was that about? The loss of faith wasn't a crisis. What had happened was a crisis.

I can see that being at such a bedside is a more sacred place to be than simply a ritual service in school. What did you learn there about the nature of life?

I can remember kneeling down by my parents' bed the day after my mother's accident, when it was still by no means clear whether she was going to live or die. I began talking to God and saying, if you let her live I will do the following things – they were all to do with work. I hadn't been a talented or energetic school child, and I did very badly at exams. But I had started to get interested in English literature because I'd just come into contact with a very inspiring teacher. I promised

God that I would concentrate harder on my English. But it was the wrong deal. It would have been better for my mother if she had died sooner.

So, if you believed your prayer was answered you would have been responsible for prolonging her suffering. Do you still feel any guilt about that?

I have very mixed feelings about it. It would have been kinder to her, and it might have been easier for us, frankly, if she hadn't lived for such a long time, in such pain. On the other hand, I have tried to do things with my life which are useful to others. I have an idea of public service which is important to my sense of myself.

Poetry has a different role in society today than it had in the time of your much admired Keats, or indeed of any of the previous Laureates, especially of the nineteenth century where it was central to their lives and not at all, as you express in one of your essays, seen as a 'sissy' activity.

Quite.

So what is the poet about today and what is he able to do?

I don't suppose it's very different from what the poet has been able to do on a good day over all the previous generations. But there is one quite interesting difference about now. We live in a happily diffuse and diverse culture and are conscious of that in new ways – ways that Tennyson wasn't conscious of, or Keats wasn't conscious of or even Philip Larkin. As a result we have a notion of poetries rather than poetry. I think about this a great deal in relation to Laureate matters. It would be bonkers to pretend that any 'public' poem

I write is written in a language that is centred enough to speak for all people in the country. It just isn't like that anymore.

Tennyson might have written *The Charge of the Light Brigade*, for instance, feeling reasonably confident that the mood of the poem was one to which the national bosom would return an echo, in a language which was broadly recognised as being the language in which these kind of things were conducted and spoken about. Well, that confidence has gone, and what does somebody in my situation do about it? I think there are a number of solutions. Mine has been to say I write poems which are pretty personal and the personal voice can sound rather interesting in a public place. I tell myself: let's hear the individual voice, alongside the voice of politicians, journalists, social commentators, and historians and see what the effect is.

Do you see this job as poet, not simply Poet Laureate but being a poet, as having a moral purpose itself?

I do in the sense that I think that literature enshrines certain humane values. What values? Well, they're to do with independence of thought, with trying to crystallise ways of thinking and feeling about the really important big things in our lives, such as falling in love, fear of death, death itself, missing people, the countryside. So yes, I do see a moral value in literature. I must say I've been very influenced in this by John Keats, who is the poet I admire above all others. The way that Keats speaks about poems in his letters, and the role that he sees for literature, are profoundly heartening. A lot of his ideas are based on his reading about literature and are generally based on his readings of Shakespeare. What makes Shakespeare so important to Keats is his refusal to come to the front of the stage and wag his finger at us and tell us what to think. Instead he puts us in situations where the moral choice is ours. We, the listeners are continually invited to ask the questions that he dramatises. That's what I mean about creating an independence of mind which is profoundly humanising.

That has important repercussions for your own beliefs about the big things in life: mortality, purpose, existence of God, life after death. You don't offer answers.

If I were a different kind of poet, I would feel able to moralise in a way which did allow me to offer an answer. But the reason poetry matters to me so deeply is essentially to do with the fact that it allows me – in the best possible sense – to be in two minds about everything.

What is your concept of God, then?

I feel confused about it. My concept of God has got very little to do with last things. It's not really to do with death and what happens after death, or might happen after death …

The creator?

No, I don't believe in that. Creation is biology and Darwin. But I believe in the value of the numinous. I can call it beauty and truth, and I often do. But there are also days now when I call it God. In other words – straight churchgoers will be in despair at hearing this I dare say – I want to think of God *in the world*. In relation to good deeds of course – but also in relation to making things. Making things which you can share with other people.

You're in middle age now. You had a health scare in 1996 when you had a tumour on your spine.

I did, yes. I thought I was going to die then, and I realised I wasn't the least bit frightened of dying. And I don't think I'll change my mind about that. Indeed there are plenty of days when I quite look forward to it, to be honest.

What do you think death is?

Nothing. The only thing that keeps me awake sweating at night is the idea that there might be something. I just want to go out like a light.

You wrote in a poem and I think it was your voice speaking in 'It is an offence'*: 'I admit that I also yearn to leave my mark on society.' What are the priorities of that, is it the public figure, or is it the private poet?*

It was slightly tongue-in-cheek, that poem, so you mustn't take it quite as it stands. But given what I've said about wanting to make things which last, I'll never know whether I've succeeded because I won't be here to see.

19

JEANETTE WINTERSON

'I am not a Christian, but I am one of the faithful.'

In 1985 Jeanette Winterson won the Whitbread prize for a first novel, with Oranges are not the Only Fruit. *She was 23 years old. She thinks of her work between 1985 and 2000 as a sequence: the first part of a journey, beginning with* Oranges *and ending with* The Power Book *in 2000. In 2004 she published* Lighthousekeeping.

For me the world was a place that was full of strangeness right from the beginning. My parents had gone to an orphanage outside Manchester and they stood by two cribs wondering which one to choose. And ever afterwards my mother always used to say to me in great disgust, 'Oh we went to the wrong crib we should have got Paul.' This was accentuated by the fact that they were Fundamentalist Christians. They wanted to dedicate me to God. They wanted me to be a missionary. That was their great hope, not that I should marry, but that I should go out into the missionary field and save souls, and that was what I was for. So they were bitterly disappointed when things began to work out rather differently.

What did you take on board initially as a small child?
We went to church every day and I did love going because

the Pentecostal movement, and that was the Church I was brought up in, is very lively. It is also very welcoming and inclusive, and it made a counterpoint to some of the coldness and perhaps the remoteness that was happening to me at home. In that sense it was a good thing because this was a place where there were lots of other adults who cared about and who would look after me. So for me to be in that Church environment I think was healthy.

And within that Church environment you learnt to love the Lord, and Jesus was your Lord.

I learnt to love. I think that is important because I've never lost it, and you have to learn to love. If you are abandoned by your mother as I was on the steps of the orphanage – all very Dickensian – then something in you will be damaged and you have to be able to love through that. So I was glad of that opportunity. That changed later when I began to be not what they wanted. But in the early stages it was their acceptance, love and knowing that God loved me, an encompassing love where I felt safe.

Was it a very strict upbringing?

Yes. My father used to beat me, because my mother used to tell him to do so. In those strictly gender segregated households, the working classes in the early '60s, men cleaned the shoes and then beat the children. And so, I would be regularly beaten for misdemeanours.

Did you carry a load of guilt? Did you feel that you were a child of sin?

No. I had no guilt whatsoever. I felt that I was a child of God, and that being loved by God I could trust myself and my actions. I think that was a great bonus. One of the good things about that Church movement is that, because it's a direct unmediated relationship between you and God, you are encouraged to trust what you do and to believe God is speaking through you.

Where does the role of evil fit in there? The Devil and all he stands for?

The Devil is always outside; the devil is always someone else. For us the Devil was our neighbours, most specifically Mrs Winterson hated next door because they were always drunk and they would come home clattering the beer bottles on a Saturday night, and they would have sex.

This is a very passionate woman, what relationship did you have with her, and what's its legacy?

It was a combative relationship, it was a very dramatic relationship, and she was a drama queen, Mrs Winterson. She never missed a moment when she could perform, and that was both to me and to a wider public whether it was the neighbours or the Church. And she felt that she was above people in the street, she felt that because she was saved, she was superior The chief difference between us is that she was unhappy and I was happy. I was a happy child.

Did you believe you were saved?

Absolutely.

And how is that defined? You saved and the rest of the people in the street damned?

Definitely damned, all of them. But they could be saved, I mean there was always an opportunity there.

When did you come to question all this?

When I was in my teens and I fell in love with another girl. At that point, everything began to change, because when that was discovered, I was suddenly outcast and damned. I had loved somebody that I was not supposed to love. It was very frightening, it is one of the most frightening things that has ever happened to me. The pastor made this terrible announcement that one of the congregation had fallen into sin of the most damnable kind. I couldn't imagine who he was talking about. And then it was me. There is that moment of absolute shock where your name is called.

How do you survive?

I had to choose. I mean it was a choice between giving up this girl that I was in love with, or giving up my home and giving up the Church. What happens at these crossroads of common sense is not simply about giving up the person; the big questions become constellated. So it was a choice not about her, but about everything in my life up to that point.

How much lives on in you now from that earlier life?

I was very angry for a while, and I think very damaged. Then I got into Oxford which was a great salvation. I used to have the most terrible rages. That's something that's gone now, but I think it came out of being both beaten and rejected.

When you went to Oxford what influences swept into your life?

Art. It had been books when I was child. They had shown me that there were worlds beyond my own, because books in our house were forbidden unless they were scriptural books, or the Bible. And everything that I had was vetted by my mother, who used to say 'You never know what's in a book until it's too late.' And I used to hide books under my bed, and hope she wouldn't find them. But my bed began to rise visibly, and she saw it, and she came in when I was at school and she took all the books in the back yard and burned them.

No wonder the books became the new Bible when you were at Oxford.

Yes. At Oxford, when somebody would knock on the door, I used to hide the book under the pillow, because I thought somebody would come and take it away. To be in a place where you were actually encouraged to read, it seemed to me that I had died and gone to heaven.

None the less the temptation to believe that all books held a truth for you, because they had been forbidden must have been great. How did you learn to judge?

I didn't for a long time. I just read everything and absorbed everything, with great enthusiasm and joy. I just ran round like crazy. And only later was there any kind of discrimination that came in, and maybe that's something that only happens when you are older because when you are young you seem to have infinite time, infinite space.

When you had rejected the Church and the Church had rejected you, where did you look for moral guidance?

I'd always been wild and I did have a lot of sex, I mean, boys and girls, because I enjoyed it, and I thought it would tell me something about myself and about the world. You have to get in there, and feel it in your own body in your own life. But I looked to the poets; I am a hopeless romantic in that sense. I do think beauty is truth, and truth is beauty. So I read the poets and I found they were not consolation but challenge. A differ-

ent world order and a moral sense which had to be personal
and individual. Which of course keyed in with the idea that
your relationship with God was unmediated. In a sense that
wasn't a switch but it was about finding personal moral
values, and what mattered to me.

*And what do you believe are the moral rules that govern behaviour
now?*

I think we are in a time of great crisis, because most people
would prefer to have a system outside of themselves which
tells them what to do. That's why the state is so powerful, and
the state is always encroaching because we like to know where
we stand. We like other people to take responsibility. And as
the Church has been driven back because none of us really
believe in God any more, the state has come forward which is
entirely unhelpful. It doesn't help people make their own
moral choices, and without that you never grow up, you never
become a full human being.

*You have said 'I made myself into what I am because it's what I
wanted to be.' How much do you feel the power of the will to
determine your life?*

Hugely. There is always a struggle, isn't there, between self
and world, in that you will either go down certain paths that
are laid out for you or you will choose your own road, hack
your path through the forest. That's it, it's very Dante: 'Midway through this life of ours I found myself alone in the dark
wood.' But I suppose that's always happening. It's not just
midway. We are always in the dark wood, and it's finding a
path rather than just being seduced by the lights that say
'Come this way.'

233

You have said 'I am not a Christian, but I am one of the faithful.' Now, although I can't quite understand it, I feel that's a very meaningful statement for you.

Yes, it is. I mean that I feel connected to God in so much as I believe in God, not the God as described in the Bible, or indeed in any other religious system, because the largeness of God cannot be contained. If the religions agree on anything it's that God is not containable and finite, and that what we know is always very partial and biased. So I am looking for something outside of all that. Part of our challenge and our glory is to live in that largeness.

How do you now regard the narrative, the Christian narrative, the Gospel story?

I still find it extraordinarily moving, the idea of the word becoming flesh. For me, as a writer, that is what I do. You make the words into something which is visceral, something which is tangible, something you can hold in your hand, it becomes talismanic.

But that's still a metaphor. I am speaking of something like the Incarnation, the Virgin Birth, and empty tomb, the Resurrection. Does that still have meaning for you?

Yes, it does. It is the sense of moving forward and moving on. The idea that Christ is pinned to the Cross, that there is the Resurrection, the tomb is empty. It is about suffering but it's about suffering coming to an end, it's about moving beyond suffering into a new kind of understanding, into a new revelation of yourself. That is glorious in the Christian message; that we don't end in darkness, we move towards light.

But what is prayer for you?

I talk to God. I talk out loud, I talk as I would talk to you now. I have this conversation and I believe, for whatever reason, that I get a response, something in me does shift. And when I had a very bad time, when I left London and went to the Cotswolds, I didn't write for over a year, the press were hounding me, it was a mess. I couldn't do anything. I went out every day, and I just sat there, whether it was raining, whether it was fine, in this state of inert darkness, waiting for something to move. All I could do was pray and say that *I want this to change, I want to move forward through this.* And eventually, it did.

Where did the answer come from?

It came from inside but it felt like there was something larger than me directing it. It felt like I was being scooped up, into energy, into a sense that my life did have a purpose. We all have these religious impulses towards what we call God, so it doesn't really matter whether God exists or not. What matters is that we are drawn towards an idea of God and that we have made a world around it.

You have recently completed seven books which you speak of as a sequence. In what sense have they nourished you and redefined you?

Well, I am always writing about boundaries and about desire, always pushing at the limits of my world, leaning on the limits of myself I suppose, and just seeing how those limits can be stretched, where the edges are, and what the tensions are between the things that hold you in, for good or ill, and your own sense of longing and of wanting to break out of all that. In my books I have stalked these problems from every side.

You've spoken about something coming to an end when you finished The Power Book, *and indeed you went through a very rough time. What actually happened?*

I was in Cornwall in a cottage by myself, and I had *The Power Book* in kit form all over the floor, because that's how I write, I don't write sequentially. And I got ill, I got a temperature of about 103, I don't know why, and time collapsed. I didn't know whether it was day or night, and this went on for seven days. I went back into a space where all my memory was accessible to me, even from when I was a tiny child, when I was in the orphanage, when I was less than six months old, I could remember things very vividly. These weren't hallucinations, they were certainly memories. It felt to me as if all that past was being offered so that I could leave it behind, it was as if to say, 'You've worked with this long enough, you can go now, you can go into the next part of the journey.' And I felt enormous energy and enormous freedom.

So do you see the books as in some way preaching?

I see them as communication, that's what I think I am for. I am here to communicate. It seems to me that my job is to take this raw material, this tangled mess that we call our lives, and not put it into any order which is artificial, but express it in a way that gives people words for things which stick in their throat, which make them dumb, which seize them up. Because, as soon as you can talk about things they cease to have power over you in the same way.

In terms of the way you have hit public awareness, you are very assertive in your statements about yourself. You have rowed quite publicly with people. How do you feel about that?

Well, I'm not as wild as I was. I'm becoming more and more comfortable with what I am, not in a complacent way, but in an accepting way, and I think that's one of the good things about getting older. If you have faced up and taken your fences, then you should learn something about yourself.

I've done my growing up in public, which isn't a good thing to do. In your twenties or early thirties, you are just making a mess, and when there are people looking at you all the time and then commenting, that can be de-stabilising. And there is nobody to say, 'for God's sake shut up', which is what I could have done with.

What did you do with the pain?

I felt it. I never closed myself from pain, or indeed from emotion of any kind. I really do suffer, I really feel things so strongly.

Do you believe that you have a destiny as a writer?

Yes. There is no question to me about that. It's not just my job, it's my work in the world. It is my missionary position. It's to open people up to the joy and the strength that there is in life, and in themselves. And to get people out of this littleness, this feeling of being boxed in, this feeling of being out of control, so that life is small and grey and endlessly fragmenting. I don't believe that is the case. I think it's a lie about life. One of the reasons I am passionate about art is because it's so large, and because it opens spaces for you. It opens cathedrals in the mind where you can go, and you can be, and you can pray and you are not small.

It's said we live in a secular world. What do you make of that?

If people think there is no God, then it's very difficult for them to have values which are absolute or which seem meaningful to them. That's the danger. I mean nobody knows why they think anything, why they believe anything, and it's going to have to be more than a humanist experiment. We have to be able to put back meaning into the lives of ordinary individuals, and doing that is extremely difficult. The word God used to have meaning. People felt that they could attach themselves to the idea, and it gave their lives validity. We don't have that now.

So but where is the renewal to come from?

Well I think it will come from art, I think it has to. Not because art is a substitute for religion, but because it taps into those same energies and is about expanding life rather than shrinking it.

Do you believe in a life after death?

Yes I do, because I can't see that all this energy simply stops. I believe that energy continues. If you look at the natural world, the whole economy of the natural world is about re-cycling, and it is also a law of physics that energy cannot be lost, it can only be transformed. So why do we think this all stops at death?

But what happens to the soul? Do we survive as individuals?

I don't think we do survive as individuals. No. I think this is just one identity among many. It's one page of a book. This world is probably one state of energy, energy moving at a particular speed, and we will pass beyond that.

Are you happy to pass into the great unknown?

Yes, because it's the next part of the adventure, and I want to go there.

20

JOHN O'DONOHUE

'Landscape is the first scripture'

John O'Donohue is an Irish poet, Catholic scholar and mystic, inheritor of the ancient Celtic tradition of poetry. He first came to public attention in 1997 with the publication of Anam-Cara – A Book of Celtic Wisdom *which was a best seller in Ireland for over a year. His next book on philosophical spirituality –* Eternal Echoes: Exploring our Yearning to Belong *– came a year later. In 2003 he published* Divine Beauty: the Invisible Embrace. *He has published two collections of poetry:* Echoes of Memory, *and* Connemara Blues.

The place where my spirit is at home is in the west of Ireland landscape. That's where I was born, in the kind, feminine limestone of County Clare and the Burren with all its beautiful, mystical shaping. In the last several years I've lived in Connemara. I love the bleakness of Connemara. It's a place of undoing. It unravels a lot of the false webbing that entangles one's mind and one's perceptions. It's a place of bleak epiphany, where many things come to light and come to clarity. So the landscape is a kind of hard, ascetic and beautiful companion, and I find that when I'm there and when my mind settles down, and I'm at home, then there are many visitations to the white page each morning.

Before you were subsumed, as it were, into your writing, you were politically active against the government in an effort to keep the Burren pure and beautiful.

That's right. In 1990 I returned from pursuing doctoral work in Germany and I was a priest then in a parish in the northern part of the Burren. And the government had a plan to build a huge tourist centre in one of the most virgin and beautiful areas of the Burren under a mountain called Mullaghmore. This mountain is a beautiful series of round shapes which have collapsed in the middle, and have these amazing curvatures. And there's no infrastructure in there. So a group of us came together, and called ourselves The Burren Action Group and for 10 years we fought the government. It was a hugely demanding campaign, and eventually we took them to the High Court and proved that they didn't have the power to build it. They took us to the Supreme Court a few days after, and we won there as well. The result of that was that we brought the government in under the planning laws to which every citizen has to adhere. We got the site restored exactly as it was, and it raised the consciousness of the environment in Ireland.

Your love of this landscape and your wish to keep it virgin has more import than that. You also talk about landscape as the 'first born of creation'. You talk about it as 'the primal living womb'. But isn't landscape inert?

I don't believe that at all. I think there's a crucial elemental choice here. I think it makes a huge difference when you come out of your home in the morning, whether you believe on the one hand you're stepping into inert space which is endless, or whether you're stepping into something that is animate and alive. I really believe that landscape is alive. I think that one of the shocking things about humans is the way that we have usurped the notion of consciousness in almost an imperialistic way for ourselves. We've cut out the whole animal kingdom and we've also cut out landscape. Now they're not conscious in the way that we're conscious. No human mind, even the most ascetic, could endure the silence and stillness that the landscape endures, and the silence that animals endure. And we are the last arrivals, the human-come-lately – a few minutes to midnight, if you take the whole thing as just one day. And yet we have claimed everything in our name and reduced it. I think that is something that has had disastrous consequences, and we're making our planet unliveable, and we're doing huge damage. The other point is that landscape is the first scripture. It is *the* wisest text, because we're not alien to it. We are the children of the earth, and the earth is in our bodies – so the rhythm that's outside is inside.

But in what sense would you say that landscape is living? Was it living and present before mankind?

I think it was finding and deepening and developing its own textures, and its own system of inner echoes. It has a sense of home in it that predates us. I know fields up the mountains where we have cattle at home – my brother has cattle – and when I go home, I'd herd the cattle for him. You'd arrive up there to these fields, where nobody walks, except for once a week my brother and neighbours. You would sense that this place has a sureness in its own identity, a belonging, and some kind of primal spirit.

Is this pantheism?

No, I don't think it's pantheism – it's the old distinction between pantheism and panentheism. I believe that the biggest theological question is – is there anything outside God? If you say there is, then you're not talking about God. So at some primal level, everything must subsist within divinity. Perhaps the actual truth is that we are so intimate, skin-close, breath-close to the depths of the mystery that if we were more conscious of it, maybe we would feel suffocated by it.

You've chosen to live alone in this wonderful setting on a mountain-side, surrounded by often quite wild weather. What can you say to us who live in cities?

Well, I think there is still a connection with the earth in cities. There is cacophony in cities, and it's there in nature, even in the midst of bleak landscape as well. You have storm, rain, you have huge fog and mist in the west of Ireland, which is the ultimate invitation to melancholia. You've all of that negativity there. I'm not arguing for landscape as just a benign presence which is the source of relentless epiphany. I'm argu-ing for it as a primal companion that has all the dexterity and multiplicity of a huge presence. I remember in California some years ago, hearing the physicist Brian Swimme say that we are of one of the first generations that have managed to success-fully forget that we live in a universe. And I think that is true. Smog at night in the city blocks out the sky and you don't know that you are in the midst of an incredible infinity.

Let's talk about your background. Father and uncle both farmers, father also a stonemason. You grew up knowing the stones in the fields round about. Your mother you speak of as the shelter of your life. Was this a devout family?

It was. It was a devout family. It was open, it was a truthful kind of family. My father was an incredibly independent per-son, an affable man, a man who, as he often said, didn't owe anything to anybody – so he was clear and independent and free. He was great fun, but he was also in some beautiful way haunted by the eternal, constantly.

Did he speak of it?

Yes, very frequently. Not in a way to make us be haunted by it, though of course that is the effect it had. But he was a very prayerful man. I'd say – and I was in religion for years as a priest – he was the holiest man I ever met, priests included. He had got there, he was inside, he was talking from within it. And often, if he was working in a field alone in the mountain and you brought him up tea, you'd often hear him praying before you'd see him. He was truly in the presence. And he had this sense as well – which I suppose came over to me – of the transience of things. He used to often say 'Life is like a mist on the hillside. It's there for a while, then it goes and you'll barely know if it was there at all.' So there was this constant focus, in a very gentle way, on the fact that we were merely strangers and visitors here.

You went away to boarding school at the age of 12. Then you went to Maynooth College, the celebrated seminary in Ireland. When did you decide to go into the priesthood?

While I was in secondary school. I was really touched by this idea of transience, and I wanted to do something that would make things eternal in some way. The two things I thought about were medicine and the priesthood. I finally realised that if I didn't have a go at priesthood the longing would always haunt me. So I studied for the priesthood with a Beckettian clarity about the Church and religious systems. I must say, while I was in there I was never disillusioned. I knew before I went in what was there. I had an amazing voyage.

Maynooth is one of the most outstanding centres of learning in Europe. It has a huge tradition, and I met scholars there who were world figures and who opened the treasuries of wisdom and learning. It paralleled something in my childhood.

I remember about at the age of about seven, one day, going up for the cows, and discovering air and distance. At that moment I knew irreversibly that I was a separate object in the landscape. And similarly when I was about 21, my mind woke up in university and suddenly I began to see that thought and perception are the lenses through which we see everything. I awoke to that huge privilege, and the frightening responsibility of trying to think creatively and critically.

That hasn't always been the legacy of the Catholic Church, to think creatively and critically. Did you come into conflict with what you were taught, or did you find these challenging intellects stimulating?

I found them very stimulating. They really stimulated me. And maybe because I had a certain dexterity with concepts, I was somehow allowed to make a natural space for myself within a fairly closed system. Because I was on a borderline, I was left alone. I found a hospitality for the things that I was opening up. When I eventually left the priesthood after about 19 years, and I was looking back on my priestly time, it seemed to me in a way to have been a time of deconstruction. For a lot of people that I ministered to in parishes, what I was trying to do was to refine their fingers. This sounds strange because it's a musical metaphor. I wanted them to undo so much of the false netting that was crippling their own spirits.

Well what is this false netting? Are you talking about the doctrines of the Church?

No, I'm not talking about the doctrines of the Church for

which I have great respect. I accepted them clearly. The things I think the Catholic Church is really wonderful at – sacramental structure, the mystical tradition, the prayer tradition, the intellectual tradition – all of which can hold their own with the best in any religious system. However I do not think the Catholic Church is trustable at all in the area of Eros. Furthermore I think that much of the theology that underpins the notion of hierarchy is bogus. I also think the Church has a pathological fear of the feminine. I tried always to open up these questions. I think a lot of the imputations of sin particularly in relation to sexuality put huge burdens on people that should never have been put on them.

Did it put a burden on you?

Somehow or another it didn't. I never believed it. Of course, when I was an adolescent I believed it. Then later on, I was able to get the burden off my shoulder.

Without guilt?

Yes. Maybe it was being a peasant and a farmer and coming into that world of theological laboratories, I trusted the native scent of my own experience more that their prescriptive ideas about what should be. Or I knew and trusted my senses.

And what about the feminine in yourself as you were growing up through adolescence and within the Church? Did you find space for that?

I think I have. Of course the Jungian psychologists say that the centre of masculine creativity is actually the anima. I really believe that when you begin to awaken to creativity, that the feminine comes alive in you in a very special way. For instance there was a poem that I wrote where I think that is, perhaps luckily, achieved – It's the 'Nativity' poem, one of the 15 sonnets in the *Connemara Blues*. It's a sonnet about birth and about creativity, but it's also about the feminine:

The Nativity

No man reaches where the moon touches a woman.
Even the moon leaves her when she opens
Deeper into the ripple in her womb
That encircles dark, to become flesh and bone.

Someone is coming ashore inside her
A face deciphers itself from water,
And she curves around the gathering wave,
Opening to offer the life it craves.

In a corner stall of pilgrim strangers,
She falls and heaves, holding a tide of tears.
A red wire of pain feeds through every vein,
Until night unweaves and the child reaches dawn.

Outside each other now, she sees him first,
Flesh of her flesh, her dreamt son safe on earth.

Perhaps you've not seen a child born, but you must have been near to birth.

I have never seen a child born. Before I wrote that poem, I knew my deficiencies in trying to imagine it. And there's a friend of mine a lovely, wild Connemara woman, who'd just given birth to a child about four months beforehand. I talked to her for about an hour and a half and took eight pages of notes. Then in the act of writing I imagined myself into it. Of all writing, I find poetry the most challenging and yet the most satisfying. A poem is the strangest threshold. It dwells somewhere in the tension field between silence and words, time and eternity, memory and possibility. A poem has no preamble; it either is itself or it is nothing. In a way it is the purest individuality of all – an utterly rigorous shape of words that dares to breathe in music.

You had been called to the priesthood, and you had a parish. But after 19 years, you closed that book in your life. Why did you do that?

It's an intimate question. The best decision I ever made was to become a priest, and I think the second best decision was to resign from public priestly ministry. There were two reasons primarily. One was conflict with the bishop. He wanted to appoint me full-time to a pastoral ministry, and I wanted time to write. I made him all kinds of compromise offers, but he accepted none – he wanted all or nothing. And the second reason was that gradually in terms of the system I was having less and less in common with it and I found it difficult to represent a lot of the positions. I'd never represented a position I didn't believe in. But I was finding the system more a burden than a gift.

It's the Celtic tradition that has furnished and nourished your language. Where does this Celtic tradition come from? Was it something in your scholarly background? Was it in your father's prayers? Is it pagan, is it Christian?

I think it's all of these things. When I returned from Germany where I'd been studying Hegel at Tübingen and returned to my own culture, I got the chance to look at it as if from outside. In the Hegelian world, and specially in idealistic philosophy and theology as practised in Tübingen, you couldn't make two moves, you could hardly put on the kettle without being implicated in some dialectical move.

And then I remember coming back home. And on my first morning back, a few neighbours came in, and I was just over-hearing, listening to the conversation. A full hour of discussion went on in which not one analytic sentence was used. Yet so many things were discussed through anecdote and the oblique respectfulness and resonance of story. And I said to myself 'There's something in this tradition.' Then I began to reflect on my own tradition and ultimately the result was *Anam-Cara*. I was so surprised at the incredible response to *Anam-Cara*: people wrote to tell me how the book had changed their lives or entered their lives at a crucial frontier of pain or loss and how it had brought them calm, assurance, courage. I never understood this as a scholarly exposition in a systematic way. What I tried to do was to make explicit some of what I consider the implicit, philosophical perceptions behind a lot of the Celtic intuitions.

Talk about your definition of the soul. What do you believe the soul to be?

It's interesting that in one of our creeds we speak of a belief in the unseen world. And I think one of the most exciting arenas is the area of the invisible. I don't consider the invisible empty. I think it's dense with refined presences, that are not coming up on the radar of our perception, our concepts.

My understanding of 'soul' would be that it is the unseen, hidden dimension of the self; the place beneath or beside or above the mind and consciousness. To put it in imagistic terms and spatial terms, I think it is the field of presence or colour or light that suffuses and holds the body. The body is actually in the soul. Meister Eckhardt says that the soul has two faces. One faces towards the world, and the other faces towards the divine, where it receives as he says 'the kiss of God'. One of the most radical and subversive things I ever read is in the Latin writings of Meister Eckhardt. It is where he said there is a place in the soul that neither time, nor flesh, nor no created thing can touch. I think that's a radical and healing insight in a consumerist culture, where identity is reduced to biography. I think that makes a space for the eternal dimension of ourselves.

But what is the relationship of individual souls to the universal consciousness? Is there such a thing?

I think there is. I think that's one of the most exciting philosophical and theological questions of all. I would see the soul as being almost completely individual, as in some sense the taste or essence of the person. I think that the most subversive thing about creation is the mystery of individuality, which is heightened in the Incarnation. So you've all these individual humans dwelling in these bodies. And then you have the world of the between, where in some strange way, without knowing it, we're all connected. And the script of that betweenness is not visible.

You speak of the individual soul and the great presence. But what is the divine?

The divine is itself. The divine is that which is totally and utterly itself. It's the cradle of origin, the primal presence – and it's there everywhere and it's in all of us. I find it so ironic that at the heart of Christianity, or indeed any religion, you have the centrality of the uniqueness of a poet/carpenter without the idea of individuality and individuation. And yet the deepest thing in individuality is actually the divine presence. To put it in colloquial terms and loosely, we're like undercover gods and goddesses, hanging around in clay form. And sometimes we glimpse it, but mostly it's darkened from us.

The presence of the divine in us is actually what creates the huge poignancy in us. We're such threshold creatures, we're neither here nor there – we're in between. If you compare, and I've often done this, when you'd be out working with animals, how at home in the earth the animals seem, and how our eyes are always drawn to the mountains and to the skies. But yet we don't fully belong there either. Humans are fascinating, precisely because of the eternal restlessness that's within them. Also they're so poignant because of their vulnerability, because they're so hurtable. Even someone who has achieved much and looks very competent and sure, even within them there's a naked place where everybody can be got to, and really hurt.

Do you ever have doubts?

Of course – absolutely. I go through Beckettian periods when there's absolutely nothing there. But I don't look on absence as the invitation to close my account with God. It's a deepening thing – I've always found it. An old spiritual director taught me in my first year when I went through an awful six months of bleakness and he said 'It's like when the seed is sown and the ground is raked and it's sore, or like the pruning, before something else comes through.' I've always believed that. And I often think when I'm going through darkness that a lot of suffering is just getting rid of dross in yourself. And sometimes lingering and hanging in the darkness is a failure to imagine the door into the light.

❖